Myths of Greece and Rome

Jane Harrison

ALICIA EDITIONS

CONTENTS

Introductory	1
1. The Gods Of Homer's Olympus	8
2. Zeus (Jove, Jupiter)	15
3. Hera	19
4. Athena (Minerva)	23
5. Aphrodite (Venus)	32
6. Artemis (Diana)	41
7. Apollo (Phœbus)	56
8. Ares (Mars)	67
9. Hermes (Mercury)	69
10. Poseidon (Neptune)	80
11. The Mother Of The Gods	99
12. Demeter And Persephone (Ceres And Proserpine)	107
13. Dionysos	112
14. Eros	117
Bibliography	120

INTRODUCTORY

THE study of Greek mythology has long been subject to two serious disabilities. First, until about the turn of the present century, Greek mythology was always studied through a Roman or Alexandrine medium. Until quite recently it was usual to call Greek gods by their Latin names: Zeus was Jove, Hera was Juno, Poseidon Neptune. We will not spend time in slaying dead lions: the practice is now at an end. Jupiter, we now know, though akin to, is not the same as Zeus: Minerva is no wise Athena. But a more dangerous because subtler error remains. We have dropped the Latin names, but we are still inclined to invest Greek gods with Latin or Alexandrine natures, and to make of them toy-gods of a late, artificial, and highly decorative literature. The

Greek god of love we no longer call Cupid, but we have not wholly rid our minds of the fat, mischievous urchin, with his bow and arrows--a conception that would have much astonished the primitive worshippers of the love-god in his own city of Thespiæ, where the most ancient image of Eros was an "unwrought stone."

The second disability is that until quite lately the study of Greek mythology has always been regarded as strictly subordinate to the study of Greek literature. Some knowledge of mythology has always been found necessary to the intelligent reading of Greek authors-- poets, dramatists, even philosophers. The scholar, even after the most vigorous application of grammatical rules, was still occasionally driven to "look up his mythological allusions." Hence we had, not histories of mythology, not inquiries into how mythology came to be, but dictionaries of mythology for reference. In a word, mythology was regarded not as a subject in itself worthy of study, not as part of the history of the human mind, but as *ancillary*, as the handmaid of literature. Nothing so effectually starves a subject as to make it occupy this "ancillary" position. To read a paragraph of Lemprière is to wonder how a subject apparently so imbecile could still keep its hold on the human mind.

From these two disabilities the study of

mythology has slowly, but only very slowly, been released by the influence of modern scientific method. The study of religion as a whole is a modern growth. So long as religions were divided into one true and the rest false, progress was naturally impossible. The slow pressure of science introduced first the historical, then the comparative method. The facts of ancient and savage religions being once collected and laid side by side, it became immediately evident that there were resemblances as well as differences, and some sort of classification became possible. With the historical impulse came the desire to see if in religion also there existed a law of development, and if the facts of religion succeeded each other in any ascertainable order.

From this intrusion of the comparative and historical methods, two religions long held themselves aloof: Christianity, as too sacred; classical religion, as forming part of an exclusive stronghold, which was supposed to stand in some strange antagonism to science. Greek and Latin religions, as different, perhaps, as any two religions could be, declared themselves one. Dying of this unnatural partnership, and of their self-imposed isolation, they at last consented to join hands with the rest of humanity and come to life again. Greek religion is now studied as a whole, not merely as mythology; as part of the spiritual history of the human race, not as the means of interpreting a particular literature; as contrasted, not as identical with the religion of the Romans.

The study of Greek religion owes much not only to reform in method, but to a very large recent accession of material, material which has again and again acted as a corrective to mistaken views, and as a means of modifying mistaken emphasis. To take a single example: the discovery and study of Greek vase-paintings alone has forced us to see the Greek gods not as the Romans and Alexandrines, but as the early Greeks saw them. We realize, for example, that Dionysus is not only the beautiful young wine-god, but also an ancient tree-god, worshipped as a great post; that the Sirens were not to the Greeks lovely, baleful mermaidens, but strange bird-demons with women's heads. Moreover, excavation, that used to concern itself with works of art only, now seeks for and preserves every scrap of monumental evidence, however humble. This has focussed our attention upon ritual. We discover and study not only the Hermes of Praxiteles, but masses of terra-cottas and bronzes, shewing the local type under which the god or goddess was worshipped; we read inscriptions relating to local rites disregarded by Homer and the tragedians.

Specially important in their influence on the study of Greek religion have been excavations on *prehistoric* sites. The poems of Homer were, as will presently be seen, the great medium through which the popular religion of Greece was fixed. Excavations, begun by Dr. Schliemann on the site of Troy and culminating now in the excavations of Sir Arthur Evans at Cnossus, have taught us much as to the religion of that great civilization which preceded Homer. Homer, therefore, is no longer the starting-point in the history of Greek religion.

BEFORE WE PROCEED to examine Greek mythology, it is essential that we should be quite clear on two points: (1) What exactly we mean by mythology; (2) what is the relation of mythology to religion?

Religion, everywhere and always, is compounded of two factors; of ritual--that is, what a man does; of mythology, what a man thinks and imagines. These two elements are both informed and vitalized by a third, by what a man feels, desires, wishes. To quote Professor Leuba, the unit of conscious life is neither thought nor will nor action in separation, but "all three in movement towards an action." Now, religion is only one particular form of conscious life, and, again to quote Professor Leuba, "conscious life is always orientated towards something to be secured or avoided immediately or ultimately." The religious impulse is directed to one end and one only, to the conversation and promotion of life.

While a man is doing a religious act, performing some ritual, he is also necessarily busy thinking, imagining; some *imago*, however vague, of whatever he is doing or feeling rises up in his mind. Why and how? Here we must turn for help to psychology.

Man is, it would seem, the only animal who is the maker of clear images; it is his human prerogative. In most animals, which act from what we call instinct, action follows immediately and, as it were, mechanically on conception, follows with an almost chemical certainty and swiftness. But in the human animal, because of the greater complication of the nervous system, perception is not transformed instantly into action; there is an interval, longer or shorter, for choice. It is in this interval that our *ideas*, our images arise. We do not instantly get what we want, so we figure to ourselves our need, and out of these images so created, which are, as it were, the empty shadows of desire, our whole mental life is built up. If reaction were instantaneous, we should have no image, no representation, practically no mental life. Religion might have had ritual, but it would have been barren of mythology.

All men, in virtue of their humanity, are image-makers, but in some the image is clear and vivid, in others dull, lifeless, wavering. The Greeks were the supreme *ikonists*, the greatest image-makers the world has ever seen, and, therefore, their mythology lives on to-day. The genius of Rome was not for *ikonism;* their mythology, save when they borrow from the Greeks, is negligible. They worshipped not gods, not *dei*, but powers, *numina*. These *numina* were only dim images of activities; they never attained to personality, they had no attributes, no life histories; in a word, no mythology.

We must always remember that mythology, the making of images, is only one and, perhaps, not the greatest factor in religion. Because the Romans were not *ikonists*, it does not follow that they were a people less religious than the Greeks. The contrary is probably true. A vague something is more awe-inspiring than a known someone. So Lucan felt in writing of the imageless worship of the Gauls:

> *"Not to have known*
> *The gods they fear, adds terror."*

CHAPTER I
THE GODS OF HOMER'S OLYMPUS

WE have already said that Homer was not the starting-point for Greek religion, yet we begin with Homer. This for a double reason. First, the gods of Homer are fairly familiar to all, and it is well to begin with what is known; second, mythology is our main concern, and though he is certainly not the starting-point for religion, yet Homer undoubtedly is the starting-point for mythology.

For this statement we have the best authority, that of Herodotus. Happily for us, under the stimulus of foreign travel, and especially of a visit paid to Egypt, the great historian came to reflect on the origins of his own religion. He has left us the following significant statement, a statement which should always stand at the head of any and every discussion of Greek mythology. In Book II. of his History, he writes:

> "But as to the origin of each particular god, whether they all existed from the beginning, what were their individual forms, the knowledge of these things is, so to speak, but of to-day and yesterday. For Hesiod and Homer are my seniors, I think, by some four hundred years, and not more. And it is they who have composed for the Greeks the generations of the gods, and have given to the gods their titles and distinguished their several provinces and special powers, and marked their forms."

According, then, to Herodotus, the mythology of the Greeks, or if we prefer so to call it, their theology, what they believed as to the gods, their origin, character, habits, appearance, attributes, was not in the main the simple outcome of popular faith, still less was it a compilation due to a priesthood; it was the work of the poets. Theology was a thing "composed" advisedly, "put together" by a number of epic singers, and this process was, according to the historian, "a thing of to-day and yesterday," fairly complete some nine centuries before Christ. We have noted the traditional tendency to study Greek mythology apart from ritual and as ancillary to literature. Now, we see how this came about. Greek mythology is, on the showing of Herodotus, largely the outcome of literature. But if the religion of Greece, and especially its theology, is mainly made by Homer, what was the material out of which he made it? No one supposes that Homer created the gods, he only "composed their generations and marked their forms." What, then, were the gods before Homer?

It is Herodotus again who informs us. He knows of a people dwelling in Greece before Homer's days, and their theology, as described by him, is in marked contrast to that of Homer. "*Formerly*," he writes, "*the Pelasgians on all occasions of sacrifice, called upon* theoi (gods), *as I know from what I heard at Dodona; but they gave no title nor yet any name to any of them*." There was, then, a time in Greece, if we may trust Herodotus, when a people lived there called Pelasgians, and when his people worshipped gods who were not individualized, not called by proper names, such as Zeus and Athene, nor even by vaguer titles such as "the Grey-Eyed One" or "the Loud Thunderer," when, in a word, the gods were things, not persons. Can we believe Herodotus? Broadly speaking, we can, because, in the main, he is confirmed by philology, comparative religion, and prehistoric archæology. Among the Olympians, with whom we must now make acquaintance, we shall find gods who are obviously in part "Pelasgian."

The Olympians dwell on Olympus, a mountain on Thessaly, from which they take their name. They are Northerners. The Hellenes, who worshipped them, were an immigrant people, who came down from the valley of the Danube and conquered the indigenous Pelasgians. Homer's Achaians are but one offshoot of those tribes of northern warriors who later, as Dorians and as Gauls, again and again invaded the south, conquered and blended with the smaller, darker, indigenous peoples, and, by blending with them, saved them from being submerged in the great ocean of the East. Homer's Achaians closely resemble the large-statured, fair-haired, blue-eyed population of the north, whose blood is in our own veins. The indigenous "Pelasgians," Herodotus tells us, "had never emigrated, but the Hellenes 'had often changed their seat.'" Their first settlement in Greece was in Thessaly. "Hellen and his sons," says Thucydides, "grew strong in Pthiotis." It was these Northerners, these Hellenes, these Achaians, who led the expedition against Troy. The Trojan War was the first collective enterprise, according to Thucydides, that gave unity to Greece.

Once awake to this northern element in Homer we are no longer surprised to find his Olympus a certain forecast, as it were, of the atmosphere of the Eddas. The gods of Homer, it has often been noted, are magnified men; but why are they so very big and so very boisterous? Simply because they are, in part, Northerners. Vastness, formlessness, fantastic excess are not "Greek" in the classical sense. Very northern are the almost Berserker rages of Zeus himself and the roughness of his divine vengeance. To wave his ambrosial locks and shake Olympus by the nodding of his brows, may be both Greek and godlike, but how about such manners as "pushing the other gods from their seats," "tossing them about the hall"; hurling his son by the foot over the battlements of Olympus; beating his wife and hanging her up with anvils to her feet, suggesting that she "would like to eat Priam raw"? There is such magic in the words of Homer that we are apt to forget that these are not the ways of Greek gods, however primitive, but the rude pranks of irresponsible giants. The old *theoi* have been, indeed, considerably "tossed about" and are none the better for the process.

This northern element comes out in striking fashion in the figure of Poseidon. When the Earth-Shaker goes down to battle he shouts mightily "loud as nine thousand or ten thousand men cry in battle," and his shout "puts great strength into the hearts of the Achaians." We remember how Tacitus noted with amazement "the harsh note and confused roar" of the battle-cry of the Germans with which they used to rouse their courage. "It was not," he says, "so much an articulate sound as a general cry of valour." Poseidon takes but three strides to pass from Samothrace to Ægæ; surely the gait of a northern giant rather than of a Greek god.

It has often been noted that in their human aspect, Homer does not take his gods very seriously. "There is no god so *good*," Mr. Gladstone observes, "as the swineherd Eumæus." Zeus, on his atmospheric side, is as magnificent as his own thunder; as husband and father he is lower than the mortals over whom he rules. The nearer the gods are to the Nature gods which they in part were, the more reverent they remain. Poseidon, who is half sea and half river, "moves in a kind of rolling splendour." Hephaistos, as the divine smith, is lame, and, therefore, to the blunt taste of the Olympians, ridiculous; but as the fire-god, who fights with the river-god Zanthus, he is a blazing glory. This lack of seriousness is, in part, accounted for, if we suppose that the gods are a blend of indigenous and immigrant elements. Homer is singing of divinities, who are, in part at least, "other men's gods."

So far, then, we have found in Homer's Olympus two elements; first and earliest, the primitive Pelasgian element; next, in marked contrast, the immigrant Northern element. A third element, which we shall call Minoan, must later be added, but the consideration of this is best carried over till we come to Poseidon. In the figures of Zeus and Hera, his wife, we shall see clearly mirrored the fusion of North and South, of Hellene and Pelasgian. We begin, as is fitting, with Zeus.

CHAPTER 2
ZEUS (JOVE, JUPITER)

As to the primary origin and significance of Zeus there is happily no doubt. He is the Indo-European sky-god in its two aspects; he is the god of the Bright Sky and the shining ether, and also of the Dark Sky, the god of thunder and rain. When the gods drew lots for shares in the universe Poseidon, Homer tells us, drew the sea, Hades the murky darkness, and Zeus "the wide heaven." The most primitive figures in Greek theology, long before Homer, were Ouranos and Gaia, Heaven and Earth; and of Ouranos Zeus had preserved many characteristics. Accordingly, in Homer's pantheon, Zeus, before all things, is the Loud-Thunderer, the Cloud-Gatherer; "he lighteneth, fashioning either a rain unspeakable or hail or snow, when the flakes sprinkle the ploughed lands." He has for his messenger Iris the Rainbow.

These traits, appropriate to the elemental sky-god, are a little difficult to fit in with the moral characteristics of the model father, husband, and ruler, and assuredly the human Zeus of Homer cannot command our admiration. He is apt, as we have seen, to behave like the uncontrolled thunderstorm he once was. He explodes automatically at the smallest opposition. Moreover, he is shamelessly licentious, he bullies and maltreats his wife. Yet there are beginnings of better things. He has his kindly aspect as god of strangers, beggars, and suppliants generally.

For his complete moralization the figure of Zeus had to await the genius of Æschylus. To Æschylus Zeus was at once the mysterious power that moves the universe and the moral solution of all-world problems. He cries: "Zeus, our Unknown, whom, since so to be called is his pleasure, I so address. When I ponder upon all things I can conjecture naught but Zeus to fit the need, if the burden of vanity is in very truth to be cast from the soul." And again: "Never, never shall mortal counsels overpass the harmony of Zeus." This is, indeed, a far cry from the elemental thunderstorm.

It is not, however, only the genius of Æschylus that has enlarged, softened, and beautified the conception of Zeus, till his elemental form is almost wholly lost. Pheidias, in the great chryselephantine statue of Zeus at Olympia, embodied the ideas of the time of Æschylus, and Quintilian, in discussing this image, makes this notable statement: "Its beauty seems to have added something to revealed religion." Dio Chrysostom wrote as follows:

"Our Zeus is peaceful and altogether mild, as the guardian of Hellas when she is of one mind and not distraught with faction, an image gentle and august in perfect form, one who is the giver of life and breath and every good gift, the common father and saviour and guardian of mankind. The image brought to the troubled heart of the beholder something of its own large repose. 'If there be any of mortals whatsoever that is heavy laden in spirit, having suffered sorely many sorrows and calamities in his life, nor yet winning for himself sweet sleep, even such an one, methinks, standing before the image of the god, would forget all things whatsoever in his mortal life hard to be endured, so wondrously hast thou Pheidias, conceived and wrought it, and such grace and light shine upon it from thy art.'"

Such is the life history of Zeus from thunderstorm to Paraclete.

CHAPTER 3
HERA

We pass to Hera, wife of Zeus. At first Hera seems all wife, the great typical bride, and the sacred marriage of Zeus and Hera seems the prototype of human wedlock. So Homer, no doubt, intended us to think, but, if this is really the case what means the ceaseless, turbulent, hostility between Zeus and Hera, the unending, unseemly strife between the Father of gods and men and the woman whom he cannot even beat into submission? Is this tyrannous mistress really made by the Greek housewife even of the Homeric days in her own image? Moreover, at Olympia, where, in historic days, Zeus ruled supreme, Hera had her ancient separate sanctuary, the Heraion, the building of which long predated that of Zeus. At Argos, too, there was an ancient Heraion sacred to the ox-eyed goddess. In Thessaly, in the ancient Argonautic legend, Hera is queen and patron of the hero Jason. Of Zeus we hear nothing. What does it all mean? The answer is clear enough: Hera has been forcibly married, she is an ancient Pelasgian divinity, and when Zeus, the god of the immigrant Achaians, conquers her land, he marries the native princess. But she is never really subject to him. She leaves a wife's submission to the shadowy double of Zeus, Dione. In a word, the unseemly squabblings between Zeus and Hera are the outcome, not of conjugal jealousy, but of racial rivalry. Hera remains always the turbulent, native princess, coerced, but never really subdued by the alien conqueror.

Hera, then, was Queen in Greece long before the coming of the Achaian Zeus. In those early Pelasgian days, who and what was she? Her name tells us. Hera is Yār-a, the year. Hera is the spirit of the year, the daimon who brings the fruits of the year in their season. As such she has a threefold seasonal aspect. As Stymphalos, in remote Arcadia, Pausanias tells us, Hera had three sanctuaries and three surnames. While yet a girl she was called Child or Maiden, when married she was called Fullgrown, and, separated from her husband, she was called Chera, the desolate one, the Widow. She reflects, then, the three stages of a woman's life, but she reflects also the three seasons, for in antiquity the seasons were three, not four: spring, summer, winter; summer and autumn being regarded together as one season of fruit bearing. In the spring she is Child or Maiden, in summer and autumn she is Fullgrown, and in winter she is a Widow. Her winter desolation reminds us of the mourning of Demeter. This three-seasoned year is dependent on the earlier moon calendar, with its waxing, full, and waning moon.

Of all this nature-aspect of Hera as goddess of the seasons there is in Homer little trace, she has become wholly a human queen. Once only, and that in very beautiful fashion, does the old nature-aspect break through. Zeus the Cloud-gatherer is seated on the topmost peak of Mount Ida, and Hera, clad in all her splendour and girt with the cestus of Aphrodite, approaches him. "And as he saw her, love come over his deep heart." He cast about her a great golden cloud and clasped her as his bride within his arms. "And beneath them the divine earth sent forth fresh, new grass, and dewy lotus and crocus and hyacinth, thick and soft that raised them aloft from the ground. Therein they lay, and were clad on with a fair golden cloud, whence fell drops of glittering dew." Here manifestly we have the sacred marriage which wakens anew the blossoming earth in a magical spring. Hebe, it may here be noted, the cup-bearer of Olympus, and the daughter of Hera, is but her younger aspect as maiden.

CHAPTER 4
ATHENA (MINERVA)

Next after Zeus himself in Olympian precedence comes Athena, the Grey-Eyed, the Ægis-bearer. She is, in very special fashion, the daughter of Zeus; she is a motherless child, she sprang full-grown, full-armed, from the brain of her Father. This fact is never stated either in the *Iliad* or the *Odyssey*, though the relations between Zeus and Athena are always specially close, but the miraculous birth is the subject of one of the *Homeric Hymns*, a hymn of such splendour and, moreover, so instructive that it must be quoted in full:

> "*Pallas Athene, glorious goddess, now will I sing.*

*Sea-grey eyes, ready mind, heart to
    remember a thing,
Worshipful maid, Ward of the City,
    valiant in war;
Tritogeneia, daughter of Zeus the
    Counsellor,
Born from his sacred head, in battle-
    array ready dight,
Golden, all glistering. Fear took hold
    of them all at the sight--
Them, the Immortals; but she, before
    Zeus of the Ægis-shield,
Burst and flashed and leaped in birth
    from the deathless head,
Shaking a sharp-edged spear. And
    high Olympus reeled
At the wrath in the sea-grey eyes, and
    Earth on every side
Rang with a terrible cry, and the deep
    was disquieted
With the tumult of purple waves and
    outpouring of the tide.
Suddenly, and in heaven, Hyperion's
    bright son stayed
His galloping steeds for a space--long,
    long it seemed, till the maid
Took from immortal shoulders the
    godlike armour they had,*

> *Pallas, our Lady of Athens. And the
> counsellor Zeus was glad.
> Then hail thou thus, to whom, with
> the Father, the shield belongs;
> But I will make mention of thee yet
> again in my holy songs."*

The east pediment of the Parthenon, the sculptures of which that remain are now in the British Museum, is but the Homeric Hymn to Athena translated into stone. Helios, with his four-horse chariot, is just emerging at dawn, beating up against the figure of the mountain god Olympus. Close to Olympus are seated the two Horæ, who guard the gates of heaven. In the opposite angle are seated Gaia and Thalassa, Earth and Sea, half-rising from their seats in amazement at the wonder before them, while Selene, the Moon, riding her horse, sinks below the horizon. The whole scene is conceived as an event of cosmic importance.

Magnificent though the Hymn is, it somehow leaves us cold. It has the impress of theological intent, of a desire to lift the goddess from humbler beginnings to the empyrean. If we examine the name of Athena, we shall, perhaps, be able to paint a picture soberer in colouring but nearer to the facts. The longer form of Athena's name, *Athenaia*, is simply a feminine adjective, *she-of-Athens*, the maiden of Athens. The Hymn addresses her as "Pallas, our Lady of Athens." This other name, Pallas, simply means virgin. If the claim of Hera to maidenhood is shadowy, it is not so with Athena. She is maiden through and through, and her temple is rightly called the maiden-sanctuary, the Parthenon. But this maiden is essentially of Athens; she could not have been reared in any other city.

Plato, in the *Laws*, says plainly that *Athenaia* is but the local Korê, or maiden, the incarnation of Athens. But, naturally, after the fashion of his day he inverts cause and effect. Speaking of the armed Athena, he says: "And methinks our Korê, our mistress, who dwells among us, joying herself in the sport of dancing, was not minded to play with empty hands, but adorned her with her panoply, and thus accomplished her dance; and it is fitting that in this our youths and maidens should imitate her." It was, of course, in reality, just the other way round; it was the goddess who imitated, whose image was projected by her youths and maidens, she who was the very incarnation of their life and being, dancing as they danced, fighting as they fought, born of her Father's head when they were reborn as the children of light and reason.

The figure of Athena cannot well have been fashioned before the Homeric poems came from Ionia to Athens, there to be remodelled and recomposed. The rising democracy took the ancient figure of the local Korê and set her as rival and counterpoise to Poseidon, the old god of the aristocracy, whose fortunes we shall follow later. In altering and, so to speak, theorizing her, they robbed her of much of her reality and beauty; they made her a sexless thing, they forgot that

> *"A woman, armed, makes war upon*
>   *herself,*
> *Unwomanlike, and treads down use*
>   *and wont*
> *And the sweet, common honour that*
>   *she hath,*
> *Love, and the cry of children, and*
>   *the hand*
> *Trothplight and mutual mouth of*
>   *marriages."*

The figure of Athena is charged, overcharged, with intended significance, yet, somehow, she never quite convinces us; she remains to the end manufactured, as a person unreal. We come nearest to understanding her if we steadily remember that she is, in fact, the *Tychè*, the Fortune of the city, and the real object of the worship of the citizens was not a goddess, but the city herself "immortal mistress of a band of lovers":

> *"The grace of a tower that hath on it*
>   *for crown,*
> *But a headband to wear*
> *Of violets one-hued with her hair,*
> *For the vales and the green, high*
>   *places of earth hold nothing so*
>   *fair;*
> *And the depths of the sea know no such*
>   *birth of the manifold births they*
>   *bear."*

a city

> *"Based on a crystalline sea*
> *Of thought and its eternity."*

As Professor Gilbert Murray has fitly said: "Athena is an ideal and a mystery: the ideal of wisdom, of incessant labour, of almost terrifying purity, seen through the light of some mystic and spiritual devotion like, but transcending, the love of man for woman."

. . .

Some little scraps of home-grown moss still, happily, cling about the figure of Athena. She has her ancient snake crouching beneath her shield. This snake was the primeval earth-born guardian of the city, and probably the goddess herself was at first imaged as a snake. Herodotus tells us that, when the Persians besieged the citadel, the guardian snake left the honey-cake, its monthly sacrificial food, untouched, and when the priestess told this the Athenians the more readily forsook their city, inasmuch as it seemed that the goddess had really abandoned the citadel.

Then, too, the primitive Athenian Korê or maiden had her olive-tree:

> *"The holy bloom of the olive, whose*
>   *hoar-leaf*
> *High in the shadowy shrine of*
>   *Pandrosus*
> *Hath honour of us all."*

Pausanias again tells us that the goddess, as token of her power, produced the olive-tree at the time of her contest with Poseidon, and, he adds, "there is a story that when the Persians set fire to the city of the Athenians the tree was burnt to the ground, and that after it had been burnt down, it sprang up, and in one day grew up as much as two cubits." Long before Swinburne wrote his *Erectheus*, Sophocles made his chorus in the *Œdipus at Colonus* chant the glory of Athena's olive:

> *"And this country for her own has*
> *   what no Asian land has known,*
> *Nor ever yet, in the great Dorian*
> *   Pelops island, has it grown;*
> *The untended, the self-planted, self-*
> *   defended from the foe,*
> *Sea-grey, children-nurturing olive-*
> *   tree that here delights to grow.*
> *None may take, nor touch, nor harm*
> *   it, headstrong young nor age*
> *   grown bold,*
> *For the Round of Morian Zeus had*
> *   been its watcher from of old;*
> *He beholds it and Athena, thine own*
> *   sea-grey eyes behold."*

And, last, Athena had her owl, that little owl whom, if to-day you climb the Acropolis by moonlight, you may still hear hooting in the ruined Parthenon. The goddess herself bore the title Glaukopis, Owl-Eyed, and on her coins, current through the whole of civilized Greece, was stamped the image of her owl. When Athena rose to be the goddess of Light and Reason, the little old owl stopped hunting mice in the Parthenon, and mounted with Athena to be her Bird of Wisdom.

CHAPTER 5
APHRODITE (VENUS)

In marked contrast to Athena stands the next of our local Korês translated to Olympus, Aphrodite. Aphrodite is manifestly in Olympus an outsider. She belongs, as her titles tell, to the southern and eastern islands of the Greek archipelago: she is Cythereia, she of Cythêra; and Cypria, she of Cyprus, where at Paphos she had her great sanctuary. Living in islands her way was ever on the sea. As the Hymn in her honour says:

> "The west wind breathed to Cyprus
> and lifted her tenderly
> And bore her down the billow and the
> stream of the sounding sea
> In a cup of delicate foam. And the
> Hours in wreaths of gold

> *Uprose in joy as she came, and laid on*
>   *her fold on fold*
> *Fragrant raiment immortal, and a*
>   *crown on the deathless head."*

When, in the *Lay of Demodocus*, Aphrodite is released from the disgraceful bonds in which she and Ares were imprisoned, she rose up

> *"And fast away fled she,*
> *Aphrodite, lover of laughter, to Cyprus*
>   *over the sea,*
> *To the pleasant shores of Paphos, and*
>   *the incensed altar-stone,*
> *Where the Graces washed her body,*
>   *and shed sweet balm thereon,*
> *Ambrosial balm that shineth on the*
>   *gods that wax not old,*
> *And wrapped her in lovely raiment, a*
>   *wonder to behold."*

Aphrodite, we see, is constantly attended by the Horæ, the seasons, and she, like Hera, is herself a seasonal goddess. She is not, in our sense, virginal, but a korê, a maiden, she assuredly is in her eternal youth and radiance. Perhaps the best title for her is *Nymphê*, Bride. The ancients, in their wisdom, saw that virginity was not a virtue to be lost once for all, but a grace to be perennially renewed. Aphrodite is a bride of the old order, she is never wife, she can never tolerate permanent patriarchal wedlock. Her will is always turned toward love rather than marriage. When she is admitted to the patriarchal Olympus, an attempt, foolish and futile, is made to fit her out with a husband, the craftsman, Hephaistos. The figure of Hephaistos in Homer is always contemptible, but it serves to show that the Achaians had reached in their conquest the volcanic island of Lemnos, whose craftsman god they affiliated. As bride of Hephaistos, Aphrodite is also called Charis, Grace. She is the Charis of physical charm and beauty incarnate. But in the cold, austere North, where Artemis loved to dwell, she is never really at home. She has about her too much of the physical joy of life ever to find an abiding home far from the sunshine.

Another note of her late affiliation as an Olympian barely tolerated, always glad to escape, is that in the *Iliad* she is a departmental goddess, her sphere is that of one human passion. In the Homeric Hymn she is of far wider import. The poet tells how, when she was seeking the shepherd Anchises, "To many fountained Ida she came, mother of wild beasts, and made straight for the steading through the mountain, while behind her came fawning the beasts, grey wolves and lions fiery-eyed and bears and swift pards, insatiate pursuers of the roe-deer. Glad was she at the sight of them and sent desire into their breasts, and they went coupling two by two in the shadowy dells." She is here the impulse of life to all things on the wide earth, a veritable Lady-of-the-Wild-Things. Yes, and she is Lady, too, of the upper air as well as of sea and land. On a vase-painting in the British Museum, a design of marvellous beauty, we see her seated sedately on a great swan sailing through the upper air.

We are very near here to the august image of Venus Genetrix, fashioned by the Roman poet and philosopher, Lucretius. His words are stiff and majestic as became a Roman, but his thoughts are all Greek:

> *"Of Rome the Mother, of men and gods*
> *   the pleasure,*
> *Fostering Venus, under heaven's*
> *   gliding signs;*
> *Thou the ship-bearing sea, fruit-*
> *   bearing land*
> *Still hauntest, since by thee each living*
> *   thing*
> *Takes life and birth, and sees the light*
> *   of the sun.*

> *Thee, goddess, the winds fly from, thee the clouds*
> *And thine approach; for thee the dædal earth*
> *Sends up sweet flowers, the ocean levels smile,*
> *And heaven shines with floods of light appeased.*
> *Thou, since alone thou rulest all the world,*
> *Nor without thee can any living thing*
> *Win to the shores of light and joy and love,*
> *Goddess, bid thou throughout the seas and land*
> *The works of furious war quieted cease."*

In this image, Venus Genetrix, we have all the old radiance of Aphrodite, but sobered, somehow, grave with the hauntings of earlier goddesses.

WE HAVE EXAMINED the figures of three of the local Pelasgian Korai, or Maidens, who became goddesses in Olympus; Hera, Athena, and Aphrodite. It may help to their better understanding if we look for a moment at a myth in which they all appear together. There is, perhaps, no Greek story more familiar, more widely popular, than the Judgment of Paris.

> *"Goddesses three to Ida came,*
> *Immortal strife to settle there,*
> *Which was the fairest of the three,*
> *And which the prize of beauty should*
>   *wear.*
> *Evoê--wonderful ways have these god-*
> *desses now and then,*
> *Evoê--wonderful ways for beguiling*
> *the hearts of men."*

The story, as usually understood, is vulgar enough. It tells of a *kallisteion*, a beauty contest. At the wedding of Peleus the gods and goddesses are assembled, and Eris, goddess of Strife, throws among them a golden apple inscribed: "Let the fair one take it." The three august goddesses, Hera, Athena, and Aphrodite, snatch at the apple in hot rivalry, and straightway betake themselves to Paris, Priam's son, the young shepherd-prince for judgment.

I had been collecting instances of the Judgment of Paris in the museums of Europe for many weeks when a singular fact struck me. In, at least, three-fourths of the vases on which the "Judgment" was depicted, there was no judge, no Paris. Moreover, in no single instance did the golden apple appear. Clearly in the fifth and sixth centuries B.C., to which these vases belong, the apple was unknown, and the figure of Paris non-essential. The ordinary way of representing the myth was to depict the three goddesses walking in solemn procession behind Hermes. Moreover, the three rivals are, in the earlier vases, barely differentiated; indeed, on one vase they have dispassionately attired themselves in one huge cloak! Only in one instance can we find any hint of preparation for a beauty contest. This instance is on a vase in the Bibliothèque Nationale in Paris, and, though late in style, is so charming that it may be briefly described. The young Phrygian shepherd occupies the centre, and round him are grouped the goddesses engaged in their toilette for the judgment. Hera is putting her veil in order before a mirror, and looks well content with her own image. Aphrodite stretches out her white arm, and upon it a love-god is fastening a bracelet. Athena, attended by a large, serious dog, clean-hearted goddess as she is tucks her gown about her and is about to have a good wash! Our hearts go out to Onone when she cries:

*"'Oh, Paris,
Give it to Pallas!' but he heard
   me not.
Or hearing would not hear me, woe
   is me."*

What does this all mean, this absence of Paris, this adoption by the vase-painter of the simple processional form, the undifferentiated goddesses, led by Hermes? It means that, originally, the story was not a beauty contest at all--a contest vulgar in itself, and doubly vulgar when complicated by bribery. The vase-painter knows that the goddesses are not three rival beauties, but three *gift-givers in rivalry;* he takes an art type lying ready to hand, Hermes leading the three Graces or Charities, the Gift-Givers. The Judgment of Paris is not a *decision* between others, but a *choice* for himself. And the choice that was set before Paris was a choice that might come to be made by any and every young man and maiden. Early mythology scarcely differentiates between the goddesses as gift-givers and the gifts they bring. These gifts, dominion, wisdom, love, are what the Greeks called the *sêmeia*, the tokens of the goddesses who bring them, and Hermes had led the goddesses long since in varying forms before the eyes of each and all of mankind. They might be conceived of as undifferentiated, as were givers of blessing in general, but it needed only a little reflection to see that Charis might be at war with Charis, Grace with Grace, and that if one be chosen the others must needs be rejected.

CHAPTER 6
ARTEMIS (DIANA)

Homer, in the *Odyssey*, adds a fourth to the Graces, the Gift-Givers, Artemis. Penelope tells the story of the daughters of Pandareus:

> "Their father and their mother dear
>   died by the gods' high doom,
> The maidens were left orphans, alone
>   within their home;
> Fair Aphrodite gave them curds and
>   honey of the bee
> And lovely wine, and Hera made them
>   very fair to see,
> And wise beyond all women-folk. And
>   holy Artemis

> *Made them to wax in stature, and*
> *Athena for their bliss*
> *Taught them all glorious handiworks*
> *of woman's artifice."*

The activities of Artemis lie, indeed, as a rule, rather among plants and animals and wild things generally than among human beings. There is, however, one exception. In her aspect of the moon she watches over women in childbirth.

Artemis, undoubtedly, like her brother Apollo, is a Northerner. She was worshipped with the title of Queen in Thrace and in Pæonia, and it is there that her aspect as moon-goddess is most clearly evident. There, too, she has the title of Hekate, the Far-Darter, the feminine of Apollo Hekatos. As Hekate, as moon-goddess, she has her dark and spectral side, and is compact of magic and spells. Of this moon-magic of Artemis-Hekate we have a wondrous picture in the second Idyll of Theocritus. Simætha, slighted by her love and half-crazed with misery, invokes Hekate-Artemis and tries to draw her lover back by the incantation of a wheel, to which an *iynx*, a *wry-neck*, is bound. The incantation takes place by moonlight. Simætha sings:

> *"Lo! now the barley smoulders in the*
> *flame,*

> Thestylis, wretch! thy wits are wool-
>   gathering!
> Am I a laughing stock to thee, a
>   Shame?
>   Scatter the grain, I say, the while I
>   sing;
>   'The bones of Delphis I am
>   scattering;
> Bird, magic Bird, bring the man back
>   to me.'
> Next do I burn this wax, God
>   helping me,
> So may the heart of Delphis
>   melted be,
>   This brazen wheel I whirl, so as
>   before
>   Restless may he be whirled about my
>   door.
> 'Bird, magic Bird, bring the man home
>   to me.'
> Next will I burn these husks. O
>   Artemis,
>   Hast power hell's adamant to shatter
>   down
> And every stubborn thing. Hark!
>   Thestylis,
>   Hecate's hounds are baying up the
>   town,

> *The goddess at the crossways. Clash the gong!*
>
> . . . .
>
> *Lo, now the sea is still. The winds are still.*
> *The ache within my heart is never still."*

The moon has her frightening side, she stares down on man with her cold, pitiless eye, a spectral terror charged with magic.

> *"Setebos, Setebos, and Setebos,*
> *Thinketh He dwelleth in the cold of the moon."*

But the moon has her gentler and fairer aspect. In the *Atalanta in Calydon* the chorus sings:

> *"Come with bows bent and with emp-*
> *tying of quivers,*
> *Maiden most perfect, lady of light,*
> *With a noise of winds and many rivers,*
> *With a clamour of waters and with might;*
> *Bind on thy sandals, O thou most fleet,*

> *Over the splendour and speed of thy*
>   *feet;*
> *For the faint east quickens, the wan*
>   *west shivers,*
>   *Round the feet of the day and the feet*
>   *of the night."*

And this Artemis, when she comes to slay, slays gently, mercifully. Homer, in the *Odyssey*, tells of a fair island, a goodly land with oxen:

> "With oxen and with sheep
> Well stored, and laden vines and corn-
>   fields deep,
> And hunger never comes upon the folk,
> Nor sore diseases that make mortals
>   weep.
> But to the tribes of men, when old
>   they grow
> Therein, the Archer of the silver bow,
> Apollo, comes with Artemis, and thus
> With shafts that hurt not strikes and
>   lays them low."

Artemis is, of all the divine maidens, the most virginal. Perhaps because she is a Northerner she attains an austerity impossible to the warmer-blooded Southerners. While Athena refuses marriage, she is still, in very human fashion, foster-mother, guardian, and friend to many a hero. The relation of these early and husbandless matriarchal goddesses to the male figures who attend them is one altogether noble and womanly, though, perhaps, it is not what the modern mind regards as feminine. It is a relation that halts somewhere halfway between mother and lover, and has about it a touch of the patron-saint. These goddesses ask of the hero whom they choose to inspire and protect, not that he should love and adore, but that he should do great deeds. Such a relation is that of Hera to Jason, of Athena to Perseus, to Herakles, to Theseus. And, as the glory of the goddesses is in their heroes' high deeds, so their grace is his guerdon. With the coming of patriarchal conditions this high companionship ends; the women goddesses are sequestered to a servile domesticity, they become abject and amorous. By Artemis alone among the maidens this high companionship with heroes is all but renounced. She dwells apart in lonely mountains and wild, untouched forests. She is most of all the Lady-of-the-Wild-Things.

Accordingly the local cults of Artemis are not untainted by primitive savagery. At Messene Pausanias was witness of a horrid ritual in honour of Artemis Laphria. He tells us of "a hall of the

Kuretes, where they sacrifice without distinction all animals, beginning with oxen and goats and ending with birds; they throw them all into the fire." The Kuretes, we know, are ministrants of the Great Mother, to whom Artemis was near akin. Pausanias again tells us, in detail, of the ritual of this Great Mother at Hierapolis: "In the court of the sanctuary," he says, "were kept all manner of beasts and birds, consecrated oxen, horses, eagles, bears, and lions who never hurt anybody, but are holy and tame to handle." But these tame, holy beasts were kept for a horrid holocaust, which Lucian thus describes: "Of all the festivals the greatest that I know of they hold at the beginning of the spring. At this festival they do as follows. They cut down great trees and set them up in the courtyard. Then they bring sheep and goats and other live beasts and hang them upon the trees. They also bring birds and clothes and vessels of gold and silver. When they have made all ready, they carry the victims round the trees and set fire to them, and straightway they are all burned."

Just such a holocaust was held in honour of Artemis at Patræ. After describing the altar, surrounded by a circle of green logs of wood and approached by an inclined plane made of earth, he tells of the procession of the virgin priestess in a car drawn by deer. Of the sacrifice itself, he says it was not merely a State affair, but popular among private persons. "For they bring and cast upon the altar living things of all sorts, both edible birds and all manner of victims, also wild boars and deer and fawns, and some even bring the cubs of wolves and bears, and others full-grown beasts. I saw, indeed, a bear and other beasts struggling to get out of the first force of the flames and escaping by sheer strength. But those who threw them in dragged them up again on to the fire; I never heard of anyone being wounded by the wild beasts."

Most horrible of all, among the Tauri, the local Artemis demanded human blood. In later days the conscience of Greece revolted, and Euripides makes Iphigeneia, doomed to sacrifice her brother, cry out against Artemis:

> *"Herself doth drink the blood of slaughtered men?*
> *Could ever Leto, she of the great King*
> *Beloved, be mother of so gross a thing?*
> *These tales be false, false as those feastlings wild*
> *Of Tantalus and gods that love a child.*
> *This land of murderers to its god hath given*

> *Its own lust: evil dwelleth not in heaven."*

It is a relief to turn from these savage ceremonials to a gentler aspect of Artemis. On the Acropolis at Athens there was a precinct sacred to Artemis of Brauron. This precinct must have seen strange sights. In it was enacted the *arkteia* or bear-service. In one of the comedies of Aristophanes the chorus of women tell how they were reared at the expense of the State. The State wisely took them in hand early. "As soon as I was seven years old I became an Errephoros, when I was ten I was grinder to our Sovereign Lady, then, wearing the saffron robe, I was a *bear* in the Brauronian festival." That Artemis herself in Arcadia was a bear does not, perhaps, much surprise us, and Pausanias tells us that one of her worshippers was turned into a bear. No doubt in rude Arcadia the bear was a much-dreaded creature, whom it was wise to propitiate. But to find, in the Christian era, at civilized Athens, a hear-cult is not a little astounding, and shows strikingly how tenacious is ancient tradition. We do not know the precise nature of the ritual, though we do know that no well-born Athenian man dare marry a maiden unless she had been consecrated as a bear to Artemis. Probably these little Athenian girls, wrapped in yellow bearskins, would dance and crouch bear-fashion before the goddess Artemis, and the little girls were safe from marriage for the ensuing year.

It would seem that after a time the Athenians got a little ashamed of the rude ritual; a saffron robe was substituted for the bearskin, and from the time of Aristophanes we hear more of the dedication of raiment than of the dancing of bears. One maiden, we learn from an inscription in the British Museum, offers a cloak of carded wool, another her saffron robe, a third her mirror with an ivory handle. The list is a long one, and the goddess, if she wore all the dedicated raiment, must have had enough to put on. She was very gracious, and disdained nothing; here and there some cloak or shawl is noted down as a "rag."

One girl, nameless, alas! but richer and more pious than the rest, offered to the goddess an image of herself, a small stone bear. A fragment of this image I had the good fortune to find when I first visited Athens as I was turning over a heap of stone lumber. One furry paw was stuck out and caught my eye. The small bear is crouching comfortably on her hind paws. She must at one time have been set up in the Brauronian precinct.

Among the Apaches to-day, we are told, "only ill-bred Americans or Europeans would think of speaking of the Bear without employing the reverential prefix *Ostin*, meaning Old One, the equivalent of 'Senator.'" Long after they were full-grown and married, these well-born, well-bred little Athenians must have thought reverently of the Great She-Bear.

The virginity of Artemis in her tenderest aspect makes her specially gentle to the very young maiden. An epigram of the *Anthology* shows this in very charming fashion. A young girl, Timaretê, dedicates to her local Artemis, as Lady of the Lake, her clothes and her childish toys before her marriage:

> "*Maid of the Mere, Timaretê here*
> *   brings,*
> *Before she weds, her cymbals, her*
> *   dear ball;*
> *To Thee, a Maid, her maiden*
> *   offerings,*
> *Her snood, her maiden dolls, their*
> *   clothes and all.*
> *Hold, Leto's child, above Timaretê*
> *Thine hand and keep her virginal like*
> *   thee.*"

Clearly here the maidenhood of the worshipper is mirrored in the goddess. The play of words cannot be reproduced in English, as korê is Greek for both maiden and doll.

The derivation of the name *Artemis* is not so clear as that of Hera or Athena. It seems probable, however, though not quite certain, that the goddess took her name from a healing herb much in use in antiquity, the *artemisia* or mugwort, known also as the Mother of Herbs and as Tutsan (= *tout saint*) or All Heal. The mugwort has fallen out of the modern pharmacopoeia. In Parkinson's *Herbal* we are told that the mugwort or wormwood possessed the power of dispelling demons; it was used in the Midsummer ceremonials of St. John's Eve for making girdles, and was called St. John's herb. The herb doctor, Culpepper, says that a hot decoction of the herb was used to promote delivery and to remove tumours. In a word, it was essentially a woman's medicine, and was sometimes called *parthenium*. Another herbalist, Gerarde, notes from Pliny that the mugwort "doth properly cure women's diseases." It is specially noted that the mugwort grew in great profusion on Mount Taygetos in Arcadia, the favourite hunting-ground of Artemis. A manuscript of the eleventh century shows Artemis in the act of giving the mugwort to the centaur Cheiron, the ancient physician who dwelt on Mount Pelion in Thessaly. The reputation of the mugwort lasted on till modern days. In the last century it was reported that a girl in Galloway was near dying of consumption, and all had despaired of her recovery, when a mermaid, who often gave people good counsel, sang:

> *"Wad ye let the bonnie May die i' your hand,*
> *And the mugwort growing in the land?"*

They immediately plucked the herb, gave her the juice of it, and she was restored to health.

Whether, as Dr. Rendel Harris has supposed, Artemis actually got her name from the *artemisia*, one thing is clear, the healing herb was closely associated with her cult. This brings us to an interesting aspect of her nature that has hitherto been too much neglected. Artemis, like her twin-brother Apollo, was a healer. Apollo, Sophocles tells us, had in the North an "ancient garden," and this garden, no doubt, was not of flowers, but of healing herbs. Hekate, who was, as we have seen, but the magical moon aspect of Artemis, had a similar garden, which Medea the sorceress visited, and of which we have an account in the Orphic *Argonautica*. It was shady with leaf-bearing trees, and in it grew many a magic herb, black poppy, smilax, mandragora, aconite, and other "baneful plants." In the *Hippolytus* of Euripides Artemis, all huntress, is worshipped by the huntsman Hippolytus. In an ancient treatise on hunting we are told that hunters must pay homage to Artemis Agrotera, She-of-the-Wild. They must pour libation, sing hymns, and offer firstfruits of the game taken, and they must crown the goddess. It is pleasant to learn also that the hunters must crown their dogs, and that dogs and huntsmen must feast together. But when Hippolytus comes to pay this service to Artemis, to our surprise he finds her not as Agrotera on the mountain or in the wilds of the forest, but in a garden enclosed, a holy magical place. He thus invokes his goddess:

> *"Mine own, my own desire,*
> *Virgin most fair*
> *Of all the virgin choir,*
> *Hail! O most pure, most perfect,*
>   *loveliest one,*
> *Lo! in my hand I bear,*
> *Woven for the circling of thy long, gold*
>   *hair,*
> *Culled leaves and flowers from places*
>   *which the sun*
> *In spring long shines upon.*

*Where never shepherd hath driven
    flocks to graze,
Nor any grass is mown;
But there sound through all the sunny
    sweet warm days,
Mid the green place,
The wild bees' wing alone.
And maiden reverence tends the fair
    things there,
And watereth all of them with sprin-
    kled showers,
Whoso is chaste of spirit utterly
May gather there the leaves and fruit
    and flowers,--
The unchaste never.
But thou, O goddess, and dearest love
    of mine,
Take and about thine hair
This anadem entwine
Take and for my sake wear."*

Surely this holy place, this garden enclosed, was the herb-garden of Artemis the Healer.

CHAPTER 7
APOLLO (PHŒBUS)

Apollo has in Olympus a position, a precedence, all his own. He is second only to Zeus. This is very clearly seen in the opening lines of the Homeric hymn:

"Mindful, ever mindful, will I be of Apollo the Far-Darter. Before him, as he fares through the hall of Zeus, the gods tremble, yea, rise up all from their thrones as he draws near with his shining bended bow. But Leto alone abides by Zeus, the Lord of Lightning, till Apollo hath slackened his bow and closed his quiver. Then, taking with her hands from his mighty shoulders the bow and quiver, she hangs them against the pillar beside his father's seat from a pin of gold, and leads him to his place and seats him there, while the father welcomes his dear son, giving him nectar in a golden cup; then do the other gods welcome him; then they make him sit, and Lady Leto rejoices in that she bore the Lord of the Bow, her mighty son."

Apollo here is altogether the dread bowman, and so, too, in the *Iliad*. In the opening scene, in answer to the prayer of Chryses his priest, the god of the silver bow rains the arrows of his pestilence against the Greek host encamped before Troy.

"So spake he in prayer, and Phœbus Apollo heard him, and came down from the peaks of Olympus wroth at heart, bearing on his shoulders his bow and covered quiver. And the arrows clanged upon his shoulders in his wroth, as the god moved; and he descended like to night. Then, he sate him aloof from the ships, and let an arrow fly; and there was heard a dread clanging of the silver bow. First did he assail the mules and fleet dogs, but afterward, aiming at the men his piercing dart, he smote; and the pyres of the dead burnt continually in multitude. Now for nine days ranged the god's shafts through the host."

But the god of the silver bow has many other

functions and attributes, and into these we must inquire before we proceed to determine his primary nature. 'Spite of his magnificent Olympian precedence, he has much the same simple beginning as his sister, the herbalist Artemis. If he can hurt, he can also heal. His healing aspects appears very clearly in one of his names--Pæan. Apollo Pæan is Apollo the Healer. The word, detached, came to mean a song of delivery from battle or pestilence or famine, a pæan, in our sense. When Apollo the Far-Darter, after raining pestilence upon the Greeks, is at last appeased by countless hecatombs, the people make ready a banquet and crown the bowls with wine. "So all day long," says Homer, "they worship the god with music, singing the beautiful Pæan, the sons of the Achaians making music to the Far-Darter, and his heart was glad to hear." Probably these pæans were at first magical charms chanted over wounds, but the meaning spread to include chants of delivery from all manner of evil.

The primary meaning, however, of the term "pæan" was simpler. Pæan was He-of-Pæonia, and Pæonia took its name from the peony flower. "Peony," says Nicholas Culpepper, "is an herb of the sun," and, as we shall presently see, it is well in place as a healing herb of Apollo. On the mountain-tops of Greece, especially in the Balkans, it still grows lavishly. The plant came to Greece from China and Japan by way of Persia, and in Japan it is still credited with portentous powers. The Greek form is the single red peony, not the double variety familiar in our gardens. The old English herbalists have much to say of its virtues, for it had found its way to England some three hundred years ago, and brought with it its store of folklore and Oriental magic. It was realized that the plant was a foreigner, and the herbalist called it "the outlandish single peony." The brilliant red calyx of the flower was no mean emblem of the sun. Though Culpepper says it is a "herb of the sun," it was largely prescribed for diseases supposed to be caused by the moon. It was good for nightmares and melancholy, and was used as a prophylactic against insanity and convulsions. The peony was under the special guardianship of the woodpecker, and he piously pecked out the eyes of those who dug it up by daylight.

Apollo, then, as Pæan, was, we may take it, a herbalist-doctor like Artemis, and, like Artemis, he came from Northern Pæonia. Like Artemis also, he had an astral aspect. If Artemis was the moon, Apollo assuredly was the sun.

The Pæonian image of Helios is a small disc carried on a long pole. It was carried in procession; just so the children in Russia not long ago were wont to carry round the Star of Bethlehem on Christmas Eve. The ancients were themselves well aware that Apollo was the sun and Artemis the moon. When the "barbarians" were invading Greece they refrained from ravaging both Delos and Ephesos, "for the sun is held to be Apollo, and Artemis to be the moon."

It happens that we know in some detail the ritual in which Apollo figures as the sun. At Thebes, at the festival of the *Daphnephoria*, or festival of the Laurel Carrying, the order of the ritual was as follows. It was a ceremonial strangely like the Maypole ceremonies that still survive to-day. The ritual object carried is, in fact, half maypole, half orrery.

THEY WREATHE a pole of olive-wood with laurel and various flowers. On the top is fitted a bronze globe, from which they suspend smaller ones. Midway round the pole they place a lesser globe, binding it with purple fillets; but the end of the pole is decked with saffron. By the topmost globe they mean the sun, to which they actually compare Apollo. The globe beneath this is the moon; the smaller globes hung on are the stars and constellations, and the fillets are the course of the year--for they make them 365 in number. The Daphnephoria is headed by a boy, both whose parents are alive, and his nearest male relation carries the filleted pole, to which they give the name *Kōpō*. The Daphnephoros himself, who follows next, holds on to the laurel; he has his hair hanging loose, he wears a golden wreath, and he is dressed out in a splendid robe to his feet, and he wears light shoes. There follows him a *choros* of maidens, holding out boughs before them to enforce the supplication of the hymns. The procession of the Daphnephoria is to the sanctuary of Apollo Ismenios and Him-of-the-Hail.

THE ASSOCIATION of Apollo with the laurel is familiar to us. We still speak of wearing "Apollo's bays." Ælian tells us that Apollo made himself a wreath of the laurel of Tempe, and, taking in his right hand a branch of this same laurel, he came to Delphi and "took over the oracle." We think of Apollo in connection with the bay as the oracular god. So Milton sings:

> *"Apollo from his shrine*
> *Can no more divine,*
> *With hollow shriek the steep of*
>   *Delphos leaving."*

But Ælian is right; the bay was not at first "prophetic," and Apollo was, to begin with, no oracular god. When, in coming south, he reached Delphi, he "took over" the oracle from the ancient earth goddess already in possession.

APOLLO IS A NORTHERNER; we have traced him to the Valley of Tempe, which lies at the base of Olympus. We have seen him worshipped in Pæonia. Can we go farther north? By the help of another title of Apollo we can. Apollo is Hyperboreios. Boreas, we know, is the North Wind, and the Hyperboreans, over whom Apollo reigned, used to be explained as the people beyond the North Wind. But the term 'Koreas" still needs elucidation. Boreas means the *mountain* wind, and the word "Bora" still survives as the name of a mountain in old Serbia, and its correlative in Slavonic is "Gora."

As regards the Hyperboreans, we have a curious legend told us both by Pausanias and Herodotus a legend that intimately concerns us. Herodotus made diligent inquiry about the Hyperboreans in Scythia, but could learn nothing. But at Delos he learned that "the Delian girls and boys cut their hair in honour of certain Hyperborean maidens who died at Delos. The girls, before their marriage, cut off a tress and lay it on the tomb, which is at the foot of an olive-tree, on the left hand of the entrance to the Temple of Artemis. And the Delian boys twine some of their hair round a green stalk and likewise lay it on the tomb."

From immemorial times, the legend went, the Hyperboreans had sent year by year, to Delos certain secret sacred offerings wrapped in wheat-straw from their northern home. The first time they sent two maidens, but, as the messengers never returned, the Hyperboreans were "very ill-content," and from then on they sent the offerings only to their own borders, and charged their neighbours to send them from their country to the next, and so the offerings came at last to Delos. Herodotus and Pausanias give two different routes difficult to reconcile. Into this intricate question we cannot enter. One thing is clear and is of cardinal interest. The story enshrines memories of ancient trade-routes from the northern land behind the mountain to the southern isle of Delos. Nothing is more tenacious than the memory of these ancient trade-routes.

And what about the secret sacred offerings? Pausanias says that no one knew what lay under the straw that enwrapped them. If anyone could have found out, the prying Pausanias was the man. The trade-route, however, yields up the secret. One of the treasures hidden beneath the wheatsheaves was--amber.

Amber the Celts regarded as the tears of Apollo, and it is probable that they believe it to be an exudation from the apple-tree. Euripides makes amber to be the tears shed by Phaëthon's sisters over his grave. And who is Phaëthon but Apollo? In the *Hippolytus* the chorus sings:

>*"Could I wing me to my rest amid the roar*
>*Of the deep Adriatic on the shore,*
>*Where the water of Eridanus is clear,*
>*And Phaëthon's sad sisters by his grave*
>*Weep into the river, and each tear*
>*Gleams, a drop of amber, in the wave."*

The Baltic, with its pine-trees, is a great amber-producing country, and very early this fossil resin was prized as an ornament. It is found in Mycenæan tombs and in the lake dwellings of Switzerland. The amber districts of the Baltic were known far and wide in prehistoric times, and led to trade with Southern Europe. Amber was carried in caravans to Marseilles, to Olbia in the Black Sea, and to the Eridanus at the head of the Adriatic. From these three centres it spread over the whole of the Hellenic world.

But besides amber, a thing in itself beautiful and magical, the holy sheaves contained another, unlooked-for treasure--the apple, the sacred fruit of Apollo himself.

The discovery of the connection of Apollo with the apple-tree, and the derivation of the name Apollo from "apple"--a discovery due to Dr. Rendel Harris--is one of the triumphs of modern research. He has traced Apollo from the apple island *Abalus*, on the coast of Frisia, over the Carpathians, through the Bora district in old Servia, down through Greece to Delos, finding all along the route apple-names as halting stations for the god. Apollo himself in Thessaly is called *Aploun*.

We do not associate Apollo with the apple, and there is no doubt that, as he came south, he tended to drop his northern tree and assume instead the poplar and the bay. But there is evidence enough. There is, first, his title *Mâleates* (He-of-the-Apple). In the Temple of Asclepios at Athens sacrifice was made, first to Mâleates, and then to Apollo. More striking still is the evidence from Delphi. Lucian makes Solon tell of the prizes in the athletic contests: "At Olympia a wreath of wild olive, at the Isthmus one of pine, at Nemea of parsley, at Pytho *some of the god's sacred apples*." On a coin of Delphi we have the sacred table of the god represented; on it is a sprig of bay, a wine-vessel, and a pile of apples; over the apples watches Apollo's raven, and piously abstains from pecking at them.

It may well be that Apollo's apple-tree had another claim to sanctity. The white variety of mistletoe grows chiefly, not on oaks, but on apple-trees, and this notably in England, while in Brittany it attaches itself chiefly to another Apollo-tree--the poplar. It may be that Apollo gained some of his healing power from the mistletoe that hangs on his apple boughs. The Ainu of Japan even today hold the mistletoe as specially sacred; sometimes they eat it as a food, and sometimes drink it as a medical decoction. They regard it as "good in almost every disease." Pliny says that the Druids called it, in their language, *Omnia Sanantem*--that is, All Heal. Culpepper writes in detail on the mistletoe, "its government and virtues," and adds "that the mistletoe is under the dominion of the sun, I do not question."

Again, we do not naturally, nowadays, connect Apollo with the mistletoe. But mistletoe in Greek is *ixos*, and, in one of the towns of Rhodes, Apollo was worshipped under the title of Ixios-Apollo--Mistletoe-Apollo. Is it not possible that, in Apollo, fairest and goodliest of the Olympians, Apollo the northerner, Apollo of the mistletoe, we have but the counterpart of the young Baltic divinity, Balder the Beautiful?

CHAPTER 8
ARES (MARS)

Ares, the war-god brother of Apollo, need not long detain us. He, too, is a northerner, but of Thrace, and, unlike Apollo, he is never really affiliated to Olympus. He is splendid and forceful, but never really respected. Like Apollo, one of his aspects was originally that of a sun-god: as such he appears on the coins of Thrace, and the Homeric Hymn-writer addresses him as "thou that whirlest thy flaming sphere among the courses of the sky"; but he is Helios-Hades, god of the setting, not the rising, sun. As such he is the bringer of death, not only in battle, but by pestilence and famine. In the *Œdipus Tyrannos*, when the city lies smitten by the plague, the chorus call on Dionysos, god of gladness and life, to banish Ares, him of slaughter and death. They sing:

> *"Draw nigh, thou and thy Mænad*
> *throng,*
> *Drive from us with bright torch of*
> *blazing pine*
> *The god unhonoured by the gods*
> *divine."*

Sophocles just hits the theological mark. Ares *is* a god, but he is unhonoured by the orthodox gods, the Olympians.

CHAPTER 9
HERMES (MERCURY)

If Apollo is, next after Zeus, greatest among the Olympians, Hermes is certainly least; he is the herald, the messenger, the servant in general. As messenger he appears in modern literature:

> "New lighted on a heaven-kissing hill."

As messenger, too, he appears in the *Iliad*. To him is entrusted the difficult and delicate mission of escorting Priam to the tent of Achilles, and he acquits himself of the task with a tact really divine. Zeus, as he sends him on his errand, says to him with affectionate condescension: "Hermes, my son, to thee is it especially dear to companion men;

go forth and so guide Priam to the hollow ships of the Achaians that no man behold or be aware of him."

"Thus spake he, and the Messenger, the slayer of Argus, was not disobedient unto his word. Straightway beneath his feet he bound on his fair sandals, golden, divine, that bare him over the wet sea and over the boundless land with the breathings of the wind. And he took up his wand wherewith he entranceth the eyes of such men as he will, and others he likewise waketh out of sleep: this did the strong slayer of Argus take in his hand, and flew. And quickly came he to Troy-land and the Hellespont, and went on his way in semblance as a young man that is a prince, with a new down on his chin, as when the youth of men is the comeliest."

Again, in the *Odyssey* it is Hermes who is commissioned to go to the nymph Calypso, and bid her despatch Odysseus to his home.

"And straightway Hermes bound beneath his feet his lovely golden sandals, that wax not old, that bare him alike over the wet sea and over the limitless land, swift as the breath of wind. And he took the wand wherewith he lulls the eyes of whomso he will, while others again he even wakes from out of sleep. With this rod in his hand flew the strong slayer of Argus. Above Pisria he passed and leapt from the upper air into the deep. Then he sped along the wave like the cormorant, that chaseth the fishes through the perilous gulfs of the unharvested sea, and wetteth his thick plumage in the brine. Such like did Hermes ride upon the press of the waves."

Hermes is messenger from Olympus to Earth. He is also messenger from Earth to Hades under the Earth. When Odysseus has slain the suitors, it is Hermes who comes to conduct their souls to Hades. He is Psychopompos.

"Now Cyllenian Hermes called forth from the halls the souls of the wooers, and he held in his hand his wand that is fair and golden, wherewith he lulls the eyes of men, of whomso he will, while others again he even wakens out of sleep. Herewith he roused and led the souls who followed gibbering in the secret place of a wondrous cave, when one has fallen down out of the rock from the cluster, and they cling each to each up aloft, even so the souls gibbered as they fared together, and

Hermes, the helper, led them down the dank ways."

Such is Hermes as we know him to-day. Such is Hermes as Homer "composed" him. "Touching Hermes," says Pausanias, "the poems of Homer have given currency to the report that he is the servant of Zeus, and leads down to hell the souls of the departed."

This goodly young messenger, with the winged sandals and the golden wand, in what form was he actually worshipped? The answer comes as a distinct shock. He was worshipped as a *herm*--that is, as a rude block or post, later surmounted by a head. Pausanias, when he came to Pharæ in Achaia, saw an image of Hermes Agoraios (He-of-the-Market).

> "It was of square shape, surmounted by a head with a beard. It was of no great size. In front of it was a hearth made of stone with bronze lamps clamped to it with lead. Beside it an oracle is established. He who would consult the oracle comes at evening, burns incense on the hearth, lights the lamps, lays a coin of the country on the altar to the right of the image and whispers his question into the ear of the god. Then he stops his ears and quits the mar-

ket-place, and when he is gone outside a little way, he uncovers his ears and whatever word he hears that he takes for an oracle."

Not only Hermes, but, it would seem, many of the other gods, began their ritual life as hermæ. At Pharæ, close to the image of Hermes, Pausanias goes on to tell us, "stood about thirty square stones; these the people of Pharæ revered, giving to each stone the name of a god." "And," says Pausanias, "in the olden time all the Greeks worshipped unwrought stones instead of images." At Orchomenos in Bœotia, where was a very ancient sanctuary of the Charities or Graces, their images were "stones that had fallen from heaven." Pausanias elsewhere tells us that the square-shaped images of Hermes were first used by the Athenians, who were a people "zealous in all religious matters," and from Athens their usage passed to the remainder of Greece. The sanctity of these square-shaped hermæ was seen in the panic that ran through Athens when, just at the time of the fatal Sicilian expedition, the sacred hermæ were sacrilegiously mutilated.

Nothing could apparently be more unlike the winged messenger Hermes than the rude, immovable, square herm. The anomaly struck the Greeks themselves. Babrius, writing in the second or third century A. D., makes the god himself wonder what on earth he was. Was he a tombstone, a wayside post, or was he an immortal?

> *"A stonemason made a marble Herm*
> *for sale*
> *And men came up to bid. One*
> *wanted it*
> *For a tombstone, since his son was*
> *lately dead.*
> *A craftsman wanted to set it tip as*
> *a god.*
> *It was late, and the stonemason had*
> *not sold it yet.*
> *So he said, 'Come early to-morrow*
> *and look at it again.'*
> *He went to sleep and lo! in the*
> *gateway of dreams*
> *Hermes stood and said, 'My affairs*
> *now hang in the balance,*
> *Do make me one thing or another,*
> *dead man or god.'"*

The answer to the god's own question might hardly have been found in Greece, but from the old Slavonic rites of Russia comes a simple solution. After they had held a sort of "wake" over the dead man, the body was burned, and the ashes were placed in a small urn and set up on a pillar or herm on the boundary line of two properties.

The dead grandfather was the object of special reverence, under the title of *tchur*, which means in Russian either grandfather or boundary. In the Russian of today *prashtchur* means great-great-grandfather, and *tchur menya* means "may my grandfather preserve me." On the other hand, the offence of removing a legal landmark is expressed by the word *tchereztchur*, which means "beyond the limit," or "beyond my grandfather." The grandfather looked after the patriarchal family during his life, he safeguarded its boundaries in death. His monument was at once tombstone and *term*.

Hermes, then, to begin with, is just a herm, a pillar or square stone to keep the dead in memory and mark his grave; in form it is identical with a boundary stone. The mourner hopes and believes that his kinsman, loving; and faithful in life, will be faithful in death. So when; the autumn comes and he sows his seed, burying it in the ground, he believes that his father or his grandfather, if duly mourned and honoured, will look after the seed in the underworld. The herm becomes a giver of increase (*charidotes*).

Nor is this the end. During their lifetime a man will go to the elders of his tribe, to his father and his grandfather, and ask for counsel in time of need. Surely, now they are dead, they have not quite forgotten him. So, as night falls and ghosts are about, he steals to the grave and whispers to the herm his question. Even if the herm be dumb, the first chance word spoken by a passerby seems miraculous. There is always magic in the dead, because they have passed into the unknown, and, when the living fail, they may have power to help. So on the herm is painted the *rhabdos*, which, to begin with, is not a messenger's staff at all, but a magician's wand. And about the wand is coiled a snake, for a snake is the symbol--nay, the incarnation--of the dead man, and creeps and coils about his tomb.

Little by little the herm takes over the guardianship of all that man prizes. If the worshipper is a shepherd, the herm tends his sheep and rams, and becomes *Criophoros* (the Ram-Bearer), the prototype of Christ, the Good Shepherd. Always the herm is guardian of children and young men; he is *Kourotrophos* (Child-Rearer). As such Praxiteles made his great statue of Hermes carrying the child Dionysos.

Exactly how the long leap was taken to Olympus we do not know. When the high gods settled in Olympus, it was not unnatural that their humble Pelasgian brother should be received as messenger and servant. He had always been the means of communication between the upper and the lower world. But when he became the messenger of the Olympian gods, he had to shift his shape; his feet, once so firmly rooted in the ground, must be loosed and fitted with golden sandals, his magician's wand with snakes becomes a herald's staff, and he himself is no longer a bearded man, but a youth with the down on his cheek, "the time when youth is most goodly."

One interesting link between Hermes and his more magnificent brother, Apollo, remains to be noted. Both are musicians. The Homeric Hymn-writer thus addresses Apollo:

> "Phœbus, to thee the swan sings shrill to the beating of his wings, as he lights on the bank of the whirling pools of the river Peneus; and to thee with his shrill lyre does the sweet-voiced minstrel sing ever, both first and last."

He and the Muses are scarcely distinguishable.

> *"When Apollo comes leading his choir
>   of Nine,"*

the lyre is as much his attribute as the bow or the bay.

In the charming Homeric Hymn to Hermes we

are told how Maia, the fair-tressed nymph, bare to Zeus the babe Hermes, Lord of Cyllene and Arcadia, rich in sheep.

"AND THE BABE, when he leaped from the immortal knees of his mother, lay not long in the sacred cradle, but sped forth to seek the cattle of Apollo, crossing the threshold of the high-roofed cave. There found he a tortoise and one endless delight, for lo! it was Hermes that first made of the tortoise a minstrel. The creature met him at the outer door, as she fed on the rich grass in front of the dwelling, waddling along, at sight whereof the luck-bringing son of Zeus laughed, and straightway spoke, saying:

"'Lo, a lucky omen for me, not by me to be mocked! Hail, darling and dancer, friend of the feast, welcome art thou! Whence gatst thou the gay garment, a speckled shell, thou, a mountain-dwelling tortoise? Nay, I will carry thee within. Living shalt thou be a spell against all witchery, and dead, then a right sweet music-maker.'

"So spake he, and raising in both hands the tortoise went back within the dwelling, bearing the glad treasure. Then he choked the creature, and with a gouge of grey iron he scooped out the marrow of the hill-tortoise. He cut to measure stalks of reed and fixed them in through holes bored in the stony shell of the tortoise, and he fitted the bridge, and stretched seven harmonious cords of sheep-gut. Then took he his treasure and touched the strings with the plektron, and wondrously it sounded under his hand, and fair sang the god to its notes."

Here we have the invention of an instrument in principle different from the lyre. The lyre is purely a stringed instrument like the harp; the instrument made by Hermes out of the *chelys*, or tortoise-shell, has a sounding-board. It is the rudimentary form of the modern violin. The *chelys* of Hermes was characteristic of the south, the lyre of Apollo of the north.

CHAPTER 10
POSEIDON (NEPTUNE)

The figure of Poseidon must be studied in some detail, not because he is a god of special splendour or beauty--he is nowise the equal of either Athena or Apollo--but because his life-history is of special and absorbing interest. In following it we shall learn much of the making of a god that would otherwise lie hidden.

One thing at the outset is notable. Poseidon and Zeus are constantly in all but open warfare. In a remarkable passage of the *Iliad*, Poseidon claims equality with Zeus. Zeus by the mouth of Iris threatens Poseidon with wrath and retribution, and Poseidon, greatly enraged, claims to be of like parentage and potency with Zeus, and counsels Zeus, if he wishes to "speak terrible words," to speak them to his own sons and daughters.

"Then in great displeasure the renowned Shaker-of-the-Earth answered her: 'Out on it, verily now, for as strong as he is, he hath spoken over-haughtily, if indeed he will subdue by force, against my will, me that am his equal in honour. For three brethren are we, and sons of Kronos, whom Rhea bare, Zeus, and myself, and Hades is the third, the ruler of the folk in the under-world. And in three lots are all things divided, and each drew a domain of his own, and to me fell the hoary sea, to be my habitation for ever, when we shook the lots: and Hades drew the murky darkness, and Zeus the wide heaven, in clear air and clouds, but the earth and high Olympos are yet common to all. Wherefore no whit will I walk after the will of Zeus, but quietly let him abide, for all his strength, in his third portion.'"

Moreover, in the *Odyssey* it appears plainly that the children of Poseidon are an impious and outrageous race, giants and Cyclopes. Odysseus appeals in the name of Zeus for hospitality, Zeus the god of strangers, and receives the rough answer from the Cyclopes:

"'Belike a fool are you,

> *O stranger, or from far away have come,*
> *Who bid me fear or shun what gods can do.*
> *For the Cyclopes heed of Zeus have none,*
> *The Thunder-bearer nor of any one*
> *Of the high gods: too strong are we by far.'"*

And when Odysseus has bored out the eye of the Cyclope, he says to him:

> *"'Then to your father, lord Poseidon pray*
> *To heal you.'"*

It was in reflecting on this antipathy to Zeus and this aloofness from the Olympian assembly that Mr. Gladstone long ago, in his monumental *Juventus Mundi*, came to divine that Poseidon was in some sense a foreigner. Unhappily, in his search for a maritime people known to the Greeks, he hit on the Phœnicians. Poseidon was certainly a foreigner, but as certainly no Phoenician. In order to discover who he was, we must examine his nature and attributes more in detail.

As to his nature, surely it will be said that is simple enough. Poseidon is god of the sea. Sea-god undoubtedly Poseidon is, though we must always remember that the Greek attitude of mind towards the sea is not ours. The sea is to us the means of abundant profit and sustenance; it is the highway of trade. To the Greek it was a barren salt waste where he might not sow or plough or reap. It was the "unharvested sea." It yielded, however, one form of nutriment--fish; and, unlike the Homeric heroes, the classical Greeks were largely fish-eaters. Poseidon was the expression of the hopes and desires of a fisher people. His trident was the fisherman's three-pronged spear.

The Homeric Hymn brings us to a new and astonishing aspect of Poseidon.

"Concerning Poseidon, a great god, I begin to sing: the Shaker-of-the-Land and of the sea unharvested; god of the deep who holdeth Helicon and wide Ægæ. A double meed of honour have the gods given thee, O Shaker-of-the-Earth, to be *Tamer of horses and Saviour of ships*. Hail, Prince, thou girdler of the Earth, thou dark-haired god, and with kindly heart, O blessed one, do thou befriend the mariners."

Pamphus, who wrote the most ancient hymns of the Athenians, says that Poseidon is--

> "Giver of horses and of ships
> With spreading sails."

In both these hymns, be it noted, the horse-aspect takes precedence of the sea-aspect. In later literature we call to mind two great hymns to Poseidon: the chorus in Sophocles' *Œdipus in Colonus* and the hymn in the *Knights* of Aristophanes.

The Knights invoke, first and foremost, "dread Poseidon, the horsemen's king." Only second do they add: "Hail, Athena, the warrior queen." In the *Œdipus Colonus*--Colonus being a suburb of Athens--it is Athena and her olive who come first, but in the antistrophe we have:

> "Son of Kronos, Lord Poseidon, this
>   our proudest is from thee
> The strong horses, the young horses,
>   the dominion of the sea.
> First on Attic roads thy bridle tamed
>   the steed for evermore;
> And well swings at sea, a wonder in
>   the rower's hand, the oar

> *Bounding after all the hundred*
> *Nereid feet that fly before."*

At this point possibly someone will ask: "Why make a difficulty? This horseman aspect of the sea-god is merely poetical. Do we not still speak of the sea's 'white horses'? The racing, crested waves are galloping, rearing steeds."

This explanation we might perhaps regard as valid did Poseidon appear only in poetry as horseman. But it is another matter when we find him so figured in early art. On a fragment of Corinthian pottery not later than the seventh century B.C., Poseidon is represented riding on a horse. In his right hand he holds his trident fishing-spear, an attribute surely not of much use to the horseman! Then again, when we come to the ritual of Poseidon, we find that horses were solemnly sacrificed to him. Every ninth year, in Illyria, a yoke of four horses was sunk in the waters. Again, Pausanias tells us that the Argives threw horses bitted and bridled into Dione in honour of Poseidon. There is here no question of the "white horses" of the sea, for Dione, we know, was a fresh-water spring.

Poseidon, then, is sea-god and horse-god. This is bad enough, but there is worse to follow. He is also bull-god.

One of Poseidon's standing epithets was Taureus (He-of-the-Bull). In Hesiod's *Shield*, Heracles says to the young Iolaos: "Young man, greatly in sooth doth the Father of gods and men honour thy head, yea, and the Bull-God the Earth-Shaker." On a black-figured vase we have Poseidon depicted in strange and interesting fashion. He, lord of the sea, is seated on a bull. His left hand grasps a fish, and behind him, vaguely unattached, is his trident. In his right hand he, the lord of the "unharvested sea," holds, with curious irrelevance, a great blossoming bough. The god seems to be just a bundle of incongruities. What has the bull-god to do with the sea and the trident? What congruity is there between the salt sea fish and the blossoming bough?

The animal on which a god stands or rides, or whose head he wears, is usually the primitive animal form of the god himself. Poseidon, who had once for his animal form a horse, was also once, it would seem, a bull. The bull was, in the fullest sense of the word, his *vehicle*, his carrier. A bull is often chosen by a people of agriculturalists. He is himself the plougher, and he is also a splendid symbol and vehicle of that intense and vigorous life they feel without and within them.

Later, however, when the worshipper gains mastery over these strong and splendid animals, and comes to trust more fully in his own strong right arm, he is less impressed by the godhead of the sacred animal, and the sophisticated worshipper becomes a little shy of a bull-god or a horse-god.

But in poetry the terror and the majesty of the bull-god still remain, and this lives on in the story of the death of Hippolytos. Poseidon has granted to Theseus, father of Hippolytos and son of Poseidon, this boon, that thrice his prayer shall be granted. Hippolytos is driving his chariot by the seashore, and Theseus, when he curses his innocent son, says:

> *"And by Poseidon's breath*
> *He shall fall swiftly to the house of*
> *Death."*

Hippolytos has reached the Gulf of Saronis when the curse falls.

> *"Just there an angry sound,*
> *Slow swelling, like God's thunder underground,*
> *Broke on us, and we trembled. And the steeds*
> *Pricked their ears skyward, and threw back their heads*

> *And wonder came on all men, and*
> *affright,*
> *Whence rose that awful voice? And*
> *swift our sight*
> *Turned seaward, down the salt and*
> *roaring sand."*

A great wave rose and swept towards the chariot of Hippolytos.

> *"Three lines of wave together raced,*
> *and, full*
> *In the white crest of them, a wild*
> *Sea-Bull*
> *Flung to the shore, a fell and marvel-*
> *lous Thing.*
> *The whole land held his voice, and*
> *answering*
> *Roared in each echo."*

"A great Sea-Bull!" There is no such thing. The imagined terror that edges in awful silence up to the chariot is the god himself in his ancient animal form.

TO RESUME: We have before us a god who, though he is not the sea incarnate, is certainly ruler over the sea--Pontomedon; or, as we should call it nowadays, thalassocrat. He is also Hippios (He-of-the-Horse), and, lastly, he is Taureus (He-of-the-Bull). Could any aspects be more incompatible? How does a god so incongruous come to be? What does it all mean?

The problem seems insoluble. It was, indeed, insoluble to the older psychology. But a more scientific psychological method allows us now--indeed, compels us--to ask the right question, and, once the question asked, the answer is simple enough.

To-day we no longer ask: "Who and what was the god Poseidon?" We all, even the most orthodox, agree that there never was a god Poseidon. There were images of him, but the god himself was not. But, though there was in reality no god Poseidon, there were *worshippers of Poseidon*, people who imagined the god, feared him, believed in him. It is not the god who comes first and creates the worshipper; it is the worshippers who, in their own image, create, imagine, as we should say nowadays, *project* the god. "An honest god's the noblest work of man" remains the profoundest of paradoxes.

"What then, we have to ask is: "Who and what were the *worshippers of Poseidon*, what their environment, and what their 'reactions,' as psychologists say, to this environment; how first and foremost did they earn their bread, what were their social activities, what the hopes and fears and joys and sorrows that took their shape in the figure of their god?"

Can we in antiquity find a people who fulfilled the conditions of Poseidon worshippers? A people, that is, of fishermen, of agriculturalists, of horse-rearers, of fat-cattle-rearers, a people who were rulers over the sea, a people, above all, who worshipped the bull. But for the bull-worship, we might be describing ourselves. We English, of mixed Anglo-Saxon and Danish race, have all the needful characteristics, Poseidon, Hippios, Taureos, Pontomedon might have been projected by ourselves.

The word "thalassocrat" (ruler of the sea) brings instantly before us the Cretan Minos. Minos is known in history as the first of the thalassocrats. His god was the Minotaur (the Minos bull). Astonishing though it may seem, the god Poseidon is, in essence and to begin with, none other than the far-famed Cretan Minotaur.

I say advisedly "in essence" and "to begin with," because I want carefully to guard my somewhat alarming statement. The Minotaur is not *identical* with Poseidon; rather he is the nucleus round which the complex figure of Poseidon slowly crystallises. The Minotaur began as a holy island bull, worshipped by a people of fishermen, agriculturalists, and herdsmen. With his people he develops *pari passu*, as we shall later see, into a great imperial power.

We have tracked the bull-god home to Crete. Was the horse-god. Hippios, equally at home there? Were the thalassocrats and bull-breeders of Crete also horse-rearers? If not actually horse-rearers, they were certainly horse importers. A curious seal impression found at Cnossos shows us a one-masted vessel with rowers. On the vessel, superimposed proudly over the whole, is a magnificent horse. Sir Arthur Evans holds that we have here a graphic mode of recording the importation of the horse. The way the horse's mane is plaited, and his fountain-like, upspringing tail, mark him as a Libyan thoroughbred. He is imported, not indigenous in Crete. This Libyan horse helps us to understand a statement of Herodotus. "The god Poseidon," he says, "the Greeks learned of the Libyans, for no people except the Libyans had the name Poseidon, and they have always worshipped him." In one of Pindar's odes, Medea prophesies the colonization of Cyrene in Libya. "Seafarers," she says, "will come and plant cities there, and instead of short-finned dolphins they shall take to themselves fleet mares and reins, instead of oars shall they ply and speed the whirlwind-footed car." And in the *Argonautica* we hear how the Argonauts were caught and miserably stranded in the shifting shallows of the Syrtes, and were wellnigh desperate, but "there came to the Minyans a wonder, passing strange. From out the sea there leapt landwards a monster Horse. Huge was he with mane flowing in the wind." The monster horse was a portent, was, in fact, the god himself. Peleus, we are told, was glad at heart, "for he knew that Poseidon himself would lift the ship and let her go."

We know now whence came the bull-god and the horse-god. Libyan and Cretan elements both went to the making of the great figure of Minos the thalassocrat, the worshipper of the Minotaur.

But, it will naturally be objected, there is no such thing as the Minotaur; a man with a bull's head is an impossible monster. Let us not be too sure. In Egypt, Diodorus tells us, "it was the custom in the ruling house for the king to put on his head the fore-parts of lions, bulls, and snakes, as tokens of royal dominion." The Minotaur, then, is simply the king wearing as a ritual mask a bull's head and horns, and possibly his hide and hoofs. The Minotaur is literally what his name says--the Minos-bull. He is King Minos masking as a bull in the hope of getting for himself and his people the bull's fertility and potency. He desires what primitive people call the bull's *mana;* he prays, like Hannah, that his "horn may be exalted." In ancient days the horn was constantly connected with fertility. On a prehistoric sculpture a woman with huge breasts holds in her hand a great horn, and we speak to-day of a *cornucopia*, a *horn of abundance*.

The potency of the bull's head and horns is not dead to-day. Among the Berkshire Morris dancers the custom of carrying a bull's head still survives. The head is not actually worn, but carried aloft on a pole. Not only in Crete did men masquerade as bulls. At Ephesus the young men who poured out wine at the festival of Poseidon were called *Tauroi* (bulls).

The bull, then, was, in Crete, the sign of kingship, the mascot, as we should call it. When King Minos wished to obtain the kingdom of Crete, he prayed that a bull should appear to him. He prayed to Poseidon, and Poseidon from the deep sent up a splendid bull; so Minos got the kingdom.

WE HAVE SEEN the bull-god at home in Crete, we have watched him in Libya become a horse-god. Now he passes to the mainland. Had King Minos only desired what was naturally his--the lordship, the hegemony over the Ægean--all might have been well. But the Bull of Minos waxed fat and kicked. His lust for empire was his undoing. During the third and second millenniums B.C. the Cretans set forth to conquer and colonize Greece. Each landing-place of the immigrant Cretans is, we find, a site of Poseidon worship, and at each and every site what are called "Mycenæan"--that is, Minoan or Cretan--remains. We cannot here give the full archæological evidence. It must suffice to state the simple fact of the coincidence, all round the mainland coast of Greece, of Poseidon sanctuaries and Mycenæan antiquities. One instance may suffice. Telemachus, in the Odyssey, is seeking his father, and he comes to Pylos, on the coast of the Western Peloponnese. He finds there the "'stablished castle of Neleus," where dwells old Nestor, "tamer of horses." Down on the seashore the dwellers in the land

> *"Made to the blue-haired Shaker-of-*
>   *the-Earth*
> *Oblation, slaying coal-black bulls*
>   *to him.*
> *Nine messes were there, and in each of*
>   *these*
> *Five hundred men set after their*
>   *degrees*

*Offered nine bulls: and then on the
   inward meat
They fed and burned to God the thigh-
   pieces.*

∼

*And to Poseidon the Protector now
Made supplication, saying, 'Hearken
   thou,
Poseidon, Girdler-of-the-Earth, nor
   grudge
Our work to end according to our
   vow.'"*

THIS HOMERIC PYLOS, now the modern village of Kakovatos, has yielded beehive tombs, always characteristic of late Minoan civilization.

Mycenæan antiquities and Poseidon sanctuaries are found all along the coast of Greece, right up to the north of Thessaly, where they both somewhat abruptly end. There, close to Mount Olympus, Poseidon must have joined the Olympians, and, as he scaled the holy mount, he dropped his bull's horns and hoofs and became the wholly human ruler of the sea, Pontomedon. But always to him, even in high Olympus, was dear the bellowing of bulls and the savour of their burnt sacrifice.

Poseidon, as has often been noted, was, on the mainland of Greece, a beaten god. With Hera he contends for Argos, with Helios for Corinth, with Zeus for Ægina. He was forced to yield Delphi to Apollo and accept Tænarum in exchange. In all cases he was worsted; only at Athens, after his contest with Athena, the two disputants were superficially reconciled, though obviously Athena remains mistress of the situation. Poseidon was worshipped by the old aristocracy in opposition to the new and rising democracy, whose patroness was Athena. Everywhere these legends show that the Minoan civilization took hold on the mainland for a time, but was ultimately ousted, in part by the indigenous "Pelasgian" inhabitants, in part by the northern Hellenic immigrants.

The crisis is at hand. The Bull of Crete has wasted Attica and Megara, and only been hardly bought off by the yearly tribute of young men and maidens. Theseus, the young hero of Trozen, after cleansing the isthmus of the monstrous sons of Poseidon, Sinis, Procrustes, and the like, comes to Athens, and is sent with the human tribute to Crete. There he drags the royal bull, the Minotaur, from his palace, the Labyrinth, and slays him. Translated into history, this means that, somewhere about 1400 B.C., Cnossos had imposed on Athens and Megara an intolerable tribute. The tributaries turned at last, and Cnossos fell. Henceforth, for Athens and for all the civilized world, the royal bull is a savage monster. *Væ victis!*

But Plato knew that this was only because events were seen through hostile eyes. Crete was mother and source of much of the civilization of the mainland, though her wealth was not untinged with barbaric excess. Minos was a mighty lawgiver, and made piracy to cease out of the Ægean Sea. In the *Laws* the companion of Socrates tries to maintain that Minos as a judge was hard and cruel, but Socrates turns on him and exclaims: "But, my good man, you know that that is but an Attic fable you are telling, a stage plot."

It is now abundantly clear why, in Homer, Poseidon though a mighty force, is mostly a vindictive one. He is an alien. He stands always for Crete and Cretan civilization, a civilization in some ways as great as that of Greece, and which contributed much to Hellenic culture, but which was not Hellenic, and could never wholly be assimilated by Greece. The Minoans were not a people of artists. With all their costly material and skill in handicraft, they lacked that austerity, that reserve, that instinct for clean beauty, which was the birthright of the Hellene.

To resume: We saw at the outset that, to the making of Olympus, there went two distinct racial elements--the southern indigenous "Pelasgian," the northern immigrant Hellene. We now have to add a third, the Cretan-Minoan. Masses of inscriptions have come to light in Crete, but unhappily at present they are unread. We cannot therefore determine with certainty to what race the Cretan-Minoans belonged, but it seems highly probable that they are of Mediterranean stock much nearer akin to the "Pelasgians" than to the Hellenes.

CHAPTER II
THE MOTHER OF THE GODS

Crete has left us, not only the divine bull Poseidon, but also another figure, even more majestic, the Mother of the Gods, the Lady-of-the-Wild-Things.

The Mother of the Gods never made her way into Olympus. Probably Zeus, Father of gods and men, could not, would not, brook her rivalry, and she was a figure far too dominant and splendid to submit to mere wifehood. As we might expect, the Cretans made the goddess in their own image. Of this we have certain evidence in a clay sealing or impression from a gem found by Sir Arthur Evans at Cnossos.

The design shows a high-peaked mountain, at the apex of which the goddess stands. She holds a sceptre in her outstretched hand, and for guardians she has two fierce mountain-ranging lions, one to either side in solemn heraldic fashion. We know these lions well, for they came to the mainland to protect the great gate of the citadel of Mycenæ. Between them, at Mycenæ, is a column which represents the goddess. But here in the Cretan sealing she is no dead column, she has come to life, dominant, imperious. The Mycenæan women have, indeed, made their goddess in their own image; wild thing though she is, they have clad her in their own grotesque skirt with its manifold flounces.

The goddess is dominant indeed, but the holy bull is not forgotten. Behind the Mountain Mother on the gem is a shrine of "Mycenæan" pattern, with its odd columns and horns. These last mark a cult whose divinity was a bull-headed man, whose chief sacrifice was a bull. Before the goddess stands a worshipper rapt in ecstasy.

On this seal impression we have the Lady-of-the-Wild-Things with her lions. A Minoan intaglio, found quite recently at Thisbe, in Bœotia, gives another aspect of the goddess wholly different, but not less important. The goddess is depicted, not on her mountain, but rising out of the ground, in which she is still sunk knee-deep. She wears the Cretan flounced skirt and a short-sleeved bodice, from which emerge two great breasts. She is altogether the mother. To either side of her are, not her lions, but two great blossoming plants, also rising from the ground. In her left hand she grasps three poppy capsules. The poppy, with its countless seeds, is always the emblem of fertility. Over her right shoulder are seen the heads of three snakes. Her right wrist is grasped by a male attendant, who lifts her from the ground. It is the Mother goddess rising from the earth in the spring. The scene depicted is what the Greeks called the *Anodos* (up-rising). This *Anodos* was known to us on countless Greek vases, but till the Thisbe gem was discovered we never knew that the origin of the *Anodos* was to be found in Crete. At Delphi, at Athens, and at Megara, the Greeks had rites of summoning or calling up the Goddess. One of these rites was called the "Bringing-up of Semele." Semele, as we shall presently see, is only the Thracian form of Gê or Gaia, the Earth.

It is strange and very instructive to turn from the Olympian patriarchal, Father of gods and men, to the Great Mother. Zeus succeeded, to a large extent, in effacing her, but, in the background, her impressive figure always remained. The priestesses at the ancient oracular shine of Dodona include her name in their chanted litany:

> *"Earth sends up fruits, so praise we*
> *Earth the Mother."*

And at Delphi the priestess began her formal ritual address to the gods thus:

> *"First in my prayer before all other*
> *gods,*
> *I call on Earth, primeval prophetess."*

Gaia was at Delphi before Poseidon, before Dionysos, before even Apollo.

Our religion teaches us to revere a male Trinity; the figure of the Mother is absent. The Roman and Orthodox churches with a more happy and genial humanism, include the Mother who is also the Maid. In Greece the Mother and the Father gods are characteristic of the two main theological strata, the Mother is "Pelasgian" and Minoan, the Father Indo-European--that is, Hellenic. The Mother is accompanied usually by a male attendant, either son or lover, but his position is always strictly subordinate. We have seen how this relation survives in the guardianship of Athena, Hera, Artemis over their heroes.

. . .

THE FIGURE HALF rising from the earth we are accustomed to call either Earth or the Mother. But on one vase in the Ashmolean Museum, in Oxford, the uprising figure is inscribed *Pandora*. Pandora is familiar to us all from the story of Hesiod. In the *Works and Days* he thus recounts the making of Pandora:

> "He spake, and they did the will of
>   Zeus, son of Kronos, the Lord;
> For straightway the Halting One, the
>   Famous, at his word
> Took clay and moulded an image, in
>   form of a maiden fair,
> And Athene, the grey-eyed goddess,
>   girt her, and decked her hair.
> And about her the Graces divine and
>   our Lady Persuasion set
> Bracelets of gold on her flesh; and
>   about her others yet,
> The Hours, with their beautiful hair,
>   twined wreaths of blossoms of
>   spring,
> While Pallas Athene still ordered her
>   decking in everything.
> Then put the Argus-slayer, the marshal of souls to their place,

> *Tricks and flattering words in her bo-*
> *   som, and thievish ways.*
> *He wrought by the will of Zeus, the*
> *   Loud-thundering, giving her*
> *   voice,*
> *Spokesman of gods, that he is, and for*
> *   name of her this was his choice,*
> *PANDORA, because in Olympos the*
> *   gods joined together them,*
> *And all of them gave her, a gift, a*
> *   sorrow to covetous men."*

"Pandora's box" has become proverbial, but the word *pithos*, used by Hesiod, does not mean box at all, it means a huge earthenware jar. Rows of these *pithoi* buried deep in the earth have come to light at Cnossos. They were used for the storage of oil and wine and grain. They were also used for purposes of burial, and occasionally gave shelter to human beings. The famous tub of Diogenes was a *pithos*. When Pandora opens her box it is not the light-minded woman temptress letting out woes and ills to mortal man; it is the great Earth Mother who opens her *pithos*, her storehouse of grain and fruit for her children. In the "making of Pandora" the Great Mother has become the temptress maid, a bane and not a blessing. Through all the charm and glamour of Hesiod's verse there is an ugly glint of theological malice. He is all for the Father, and the Father will have no Great Earth Mother in his cloud-capped, man-made Olympus. So she who made all things has become the slave of man, his lure, his plaything, dowered only with a slave's bodily beauty and blandishments. The birth of the first woman is but a huge Olympian joke to Zeus, the arch patriarchal bourgeois. "He spake, and the Sire of men and of gods immortal laughed."

But we will not part from the Mother with a patriarchal joke. Rather let the Homeric Hymn-writer chant her praises:

"Concerning Earth, the mother of all, shall I sing, firm Earth, eldest of gods, that nourishes all things in the world; all things that fare on the sacred land, all things in the sea, all flying things, all are fed out of her store. Through thee, revered goddess, are men happy in their children and fortunate in their harvest. Thine it is to give or to take life from mortal men. Happy is he whom thou honourest with favouring heart; to him all good things are present innumerable: his fertile field is laden, his meadows are rich in cattle, his house filled with all good things. Such men rule righteously in cities of fair women, great wealth and riches are theirs, their children grow glorious in fresh delights: their maidens joyfully dance and sport through the soft meadow flowers in floral revelry.

Such are those that thou honourest, holy goddess, kindly spirit. Hail, Mother of the Gods, thou wife of starry Ouranos, and freely in return for my ode give me livelihood sufficient."

"Wife of Starry Ouranos," of Ouranos the firmament, who was before the coming of Zeus. As such the mystic remembered her. On the Orphic gold tablet buried with him to ensure his safety is inscribed the proud confession: "I am the child of Earth and of Starry Heaven."

It would be pleasant to track the Earth-Mother to the mainland and show her influence on each and all of the "Pelasgian" women goddesses--watch how she gave to Aphrodite her doves, to Athene her snakes. But space does not allow. Only a few brief words must be said of Demeter the Mother, and her daughter Persephone.

CHAPTER 12
DEMETER AND PERSEPHONE (CERES AND PROSERPINE)

The name Demeter means not Earth-Mother, but Grain-Mother. So long as man was a hunter only, the Lady-of-the-Wild-Things and the Earth-Mother who, unbidden, sent up flowers in the spring and fruit in autumn, these were adequate to express his needs. But there came a time when man settled down to plough the earth, to sow seeds and reap grain, and then he needed a Grain-Mother, Demeter.

We are used to see ploughing and sowing and reaping done mainly by men, and it may surprise us to find that the Grain-Goddess took the form of a woman. But the first beginnings of agriculture have always lain with women. While the man was away hunting, woman, tied at home by her baby, had leisure to sow grain and reap fruits.

Moreover, there is another and a magical reason. In his *History of the New World* Mr. Payne tells us that in primitive America man would have nothing to say to agriculture. He dared not interfere, for he thought it depended magically for its success on women, and was connected with child-bearing. "When the women plant maize," said the Indian to Gumilla, "the stalk produces two or three ears. Why? Because women know how to produce children. They only know how to plant the corn so as to be sure of it germinating. Then let them plant it, they know more than we do."

Homer seems to know nothing of the beautiful story of the Rape of Persephone and the Mourning of Demeter, of the Kathodos or going down into Hades, and the Anodos, the rising-up in spring. He just mentions Demeter but as dwelling on earth, not on Olympus: he tells how she stands with her yellow hair at the sacred threshing-floor when men are winnowing, and how "she maketh division of grain and chaff, and the heaps of chaff grow white." But he seems to know nothing of

> *"that fair field*
> *Of Enna, where Proserpine gathering*
> *flowers,*
> *Herself a fairer flower, by gloomy Dis*

> *Was gathered--which cost Seres all*
>   *that pain*
> *To seek her through the world."*

It is Shakespeare, not Homer, who cries:

> *"O Proserpina,*
> *For the flowers now, that, affrighted,*
>   *thou letst fall*
> *From Dis's waggon."*

Persephone is for Homer not Korê, not the lovely maiden form of the Grain-Mother, but the dread Queen of the underworld, ruling in Hades. Odysseus wishes to have speech with the dead heroes in Hades, but:

> *"Ere that might be, the ghosts*
>   *thronged round in myriads*
>   *manifold,*
> *Weird was the magic din they made, a*
>   *pale green fear gat hold*
> *Of me, lest, for my daring, Persephone*
>   *the dread*
> *From Hades should send up the awful*
>   *monster's grisly head."*

The "awful monster" is the Gorgon, and the

monster's head the *gorgoneion*. This takes us straight to another aspect of the Mother. Demeter herself, mild and beneficent though she was, had her darker side. The Athenians called the Dead *Demetreioi*, Demeter's People. Not only did she bring all things to life, but, when they died, she received them back into her bosom. "Dust we are and unto dust we shall return"; and Æschylus says:

"Yea, summon Earth, who brings all
    things to life,
And rears and takes again into her
    womb."

A ghost is to primitive man always a terrifying thing, a bogey, and so the Earth-Mother, as guardian of the Dead, becomes a gorgon. On a Rhodian plate in the British Museum the Great Mother is figured grasping in her hands two birds, with human body and feet, but she is winged, and, in place of her head, she had a gorgon-mask, a *gorgoneion* with great tusks. There is no such thing as a gorgon, so there can be no real gorgon's head, but there are such things as ritual masks, ugly faces made to scare men and demons. Our museums of anthropology are full of them, and they are still in frequent use among savage tribes. The *gorgoneion* has pendent tongue, glaring eyes, protruding tusks. It is the image of terror incarnate. The non-existent gorgon monster was created to account for the ritual mask.

This dark side of Demeter, as guardian of ghosts, is expressed in her name Demeter-Erinys. Erinys is simply an angry ghost, and, as ghosts are many, the name has become pluralized as Erinyes. In the *Eumenides* of Æschylus we have the transformation of these vindictive Erinyes, these angry ghosts, these figures of terror and vengeance, into figures of fertility, holy and benignant, carrying in one hand their underground snakes, in the other, to mark their double aspect, fruit and flowers. Such was the general trend of Greek religion, the transformation of fear and ugliness into beauty and tranquillity.

Two gods yet remain to be considered. Homer does not recognize them, but, by the middle of the fifth century B.C. they have worked their way into Olympus. We find them admitted to the solemn assembly seated in the Parthenon frieze. These two gods, Dionysos and Eros, have certain affinities that make it desirable to treat of them in conjunction. Both are Mystery gods. We begin with Dionysos.

CHAPTER 13
DIONYSOS

Dionysos had absorbed into his personality two non-Hellenic divinities--(1) a god of wine, orgy, and ecstasy from Thrace, (2) a Cretan mystery god, Zagreus, who is substantially one with the Egyptian god of immortality, Osiris.

As to his origin, though his name means, undoubtedly, "young Zeus," Dionysos is essentially the son of his mother, Semele; later he is affiliated to Zeus by a rebirth.

Semele is just the Thracian form of the earth-goddess. "Zemlya" is Slavonic for "earth." We have the word in Nova Zembla (New Earth or Land). The whole worship of Dionysos is matriarchal, of the mother as well as of the son, the mother sometimes appearing as nurse. So Sophocles:

> "Footless, sacred, shadowy thicket,
>   where a myriad berries grow,
> Where no heat of the sun may enter,
>   neither wind of the winter blow,
> Where the Reveller Dionysos with his
>   Nursing Nymphs will go."

The Bacchantes are the mothers; they tend the young of wild things, and they have magical power to make the whole world break into blossom.

> "And one a young fawn held, and one
>   a wild
> Wolf cub, and fed them with white
>   milk, and smiled
> In love, young mothers with a mother's breast
> And babes at home forgotten!"

At the great ritual of the mothers all Creation stirs anew.

> "And all the mountains felt,
> And worshipped with them; and the
>   wild things knelt
> And ramped and gloried, and the
>   wilderness

> *Was filled with moving voices and dim stress."*

No wonder Dionysos and his mother did not find easy access to a patriarchal Olympus!

The worship of Dionysos has one characteristic that distinguishes him from the other gods, and is of special interest in helping us to understand the making of a god. Dionysos is always accompanied by a worshipping band, a *thiasos*. His worshipping band are the Satyrs, his mother's are the Mænads. None of the other gods have a *thiasos*. The reason is clear, once the psychology of the band is realized. Dionysos is the god of ecstasy, but it is ecstasy of the group, not the individual. Euripides said of the Bacchic initiate: "His soul is congregationalized." We have seen, notably in the case of Poseidon, that all the Olympians are *projections* of the desires, imaginations, of the worshipper; but only in the case of Dionysos do we catch the god at the moment when the ecstasy of the group projects him. This is no fancy. Plato preserves for us an Orphic text: "Many are the wand-bearers, few are the Bacchoi"; that is, many perform the rite of Bacchus, few become, or, as we should say, *project*, the god himself.

By becoming one with the god he had projected, the worshipper of Dionysos attained immortality. That is the doctrine of each and every mystery religion. No one sought to become Zeus or Athene or Apollo. That would have seemed folly and insolence. "Strive not thou to become a god," says Pindar; "the things of mortals best become mortality."

It is probable that all Greek gods were originally accompanied by a *thiasos*, and were *projected* by their worshippers. But most of the Olympians have long passed this stage. Their worship is not an ecstasy; it is a sober service of sacrifice, prayer, and praise. God and man are eternally sundered.

Another trait marks Dionysos off from the Olympians. They are wholly human; he keeps about him some vestiges of plant and animal shape. He is tree-god (*dendrîtes*), and at will he can change himself back into plant or animal form. When the Bacchantes in extreme peril call upon Dionysos for vengeance, his ancient incarnations loom in upon their maddened minds:

> *"Appear, appear, whatso thy shape or name,*
> *O Mountain Bull, Snake of the Hundred Heads,*
> *Lion of the Burning Flame!*
> *O God, Beast, Mystery, come!"*

The mystery gods represent the supreme golden moment of Greek mythology. They are caught, fettered for an instant in lovely human shapes; but they are life-spirits barely held; they shift and change. Dionysos is a human youth, lovely with curled hair, but in a moment he is a wild bull and a burning flame. The beauty and the thrill of it!

CHAPTER 14
EROS

The early form of Eros is given us on Greek vases. Round the head of Aphrodite are clustered a number of little winged figures holding sprays of flowers; they are Erotes. At death there fluttered forth from a man's mouth a little winged sprite--the *ker*, as the Greeks called it, the spirit of life. Eros, to begin with, is not love between man and woman, but the impulse of life in all living things. So Theognis:

> *"Love comes at his hour, comes with*
> *   the flowers in spring,*
> *Leaving the land of his birth,*
> *   Kypros, beautiful isle. Love comes*
> *   scattering*
> *Seed for man upon earth."*

These winged sprites, these Erotes, attend the mother when she rises from the earth in spring. Later, owing to the poignant attachments existing between man and man at Athens, Eros took on the form of a beautiful *ephebos*.

The religion of Eros has one element lacking in the religion of all the other gods; it has a cosmogony. Aristophanes tells of a time when earth and heaven as yet were not, only chaos:

> *"In the beginning of Things, black-winged Night*
> *Into the bosom of Erebos dark and deep*
> *Laid a wind-born egg, and, as the seasons rolled,*
> *Forth sprang Love, gleaming with wings of gold,*
> *Like to the whirlings of wind, Love the Delight*
> *And Love with Chaos in Tartaros laid him to sleep;*
> *And we, his children, nestled, fluttering there,*
> *Till he led us forth to the light of the upper air."*

This is pure Orphic mysticism, as different

from Homer as dark from light. Homer knows of no world-egg and no birth of Love. Homer is so dazzled by his human heroes and their radiant counterparts mirrored in Olympus that he never cares to peer into the darkness whence they sprang. He cares as little, it seems, for the Before as for the Hereafter.

Homer has only a glimmering eschatology, a shadowy Tartaros, and still more shadowy Elysian fields where great heroes and those connected by marriage with the gods go after death, but in which the common man has no place. Of cosmogony he seems to have no consciousness. The two, cosmogony and eschatology, seem to go together; both are pathetic attempts to answer the question Homer never cared to raise--Whence and Whither? A religion like the Olympian religion that shirks these two great questions, gnawing always at the heart of humanity, is scarcely worth its name. The Olympians paled, and were bound to pale, before the mystery gods.

BIBLIOGRAPHY

THE translations from Homer in this book are taken from the *Iliad* by Lang Leaf and Myers, and the translation of the *Odyssey* in verse by J. W. Mackail. The translations of the *Homeric Hymns* are by Andrew Lang, with the exception of the *Hymn to Athene*, which is by D. S. MacColl. The translations of Euripides are by Professor Gilbert Murray. For the remaining translations I am myself responsible.

Much assistance has been obtained of the following books, to which I refer students for more detailed information:

1. A. B. Cook: *Zeus: A Study of Ancient Religion*, 2 vols. (Cambridge University Press, 1954.)

2. Rendel Harris: *The Ascent of Olympus*. (Manchester University Press, 1917.)

3. Gilbert Murray: *Five Stages of Greek Religion.* (Oxford Clarendon Press, 5925.)

4. Jane E. Harrison: (a) *Prolegomena to the Study of Greek Religion*, third edition. (b) *Themis*, second edition, 1927. (c) *Epilegomena to the Study of Religion.* (Cambridge University Press.) (d) *Alpha and Omega.* (Sidgwick and Jackson.)

Copyright © 2023 by Alicia Éditions
Cover design: canva.com
Ebook ISBN 9782384551972
Paperback ISBN 9782384551989
Hardcover 9782384551996
All rights reserved.

www.ingramcontent.com/pod-product-compliance
Lightning Source LLC
LaVergne TN
LVHW032005070526
838202LV00058B/6311